Let's Cook the Chinese Way

LET'S COOK THE CHINESE WAY
The ABC's of Chinese Cooking in Detail

By
LANNIE KING YEE

CHARLES E. TUTTLE COMPANY
Rutland, Vermont   Tokyo, Japan

Published by the Charles E. Tuttle Company, Inc.
of Rutland, Vermont & Tokyo, Japan
with editorial offices at
2-6, Suido 1-chome, Bunkyo-ku, Tokyo, Japan (112)

Library of Congress Catalog Card No. 72-83674
International Standard Book No. 0-8048-1101-6

Printed in Japan

Contents

Preface: 7
Introduction: 9

Fried Dishes: 19
Steamed Dishes: 41
Barbecuing: 52
Deep Frying: 55
Soups & Combination Cooking: 62
Rice & Noodles: 72
Tea: 76
Miscellany: 78

Glossary: 81
Index: 85

Preface

This book is written for those who want to clearly understand the meaning of Chinese cooking. The aim of the book is to utilize the local products: that is, to cook the Chinese way with ingredients readily obtainable. The recipes are written in such a way that substitution can be made, without seriously altering the flavor, if certain ingredients are not available.

The most important reason for writing this book, besides the fact Chinese food is delicious in any man's language, is my strong convictions concerning the diet of people in North America and an interest in the welfare of the people. It is well known that in North America we know all there is to know about nutrition. Yet, despite this fact, our hospitals are always filled with patients either suffering from organic diseases or stress and strain of modern living. I am firmly convinced that most of this sickness comes about because people do not eat properly. For this reason I am trying to introduce Chinese food into the North American homes as a regular way of cooking. I hope that I have succeeded in doing this through the classes that I have taught at night school here in Victoria. Women who have taken the course tell me that their husbands and families are delighted with the improvement in thcir cooking. No other cooking produces a more balanced diet than Chinese cooking. For example, Chinese mushrooms are used in almost all the main vegetable dishes. These mushrooms contain nineteen of the twenty-odd known amino acids (including all the essential ones) that make up proteins. By the adjustment of smaller amounts of meat to a larger amount of vegetables, one can achieve a reducing diet without having to suffer hunger in order to lose weight. Very rarely do you hear of a Chinese person suffering from constipation or overweight. The only people who do complain are those who prefer such things as steaks and pork chops over Chinese cooking.

In the preparation of Chinese food one can often relieve the stresses and strains so often found in modern day living. For example, in the preparation of a steamed dish of "meat cake" (a type of hamburger) the ingredients are chopped very finely with two knives, one in either hand. A jolly cook would chop the ingredients with a happy rhythm and a song. A frustrated cook would chop the food with a scornful look on his face and find much relief when the knife strikes the meat. The psychologist would say that it is a way of relieving one's emotions.

I do not claim to be an authority on anything I have said, but merely present the facts as I see them. The recipes in this book are based on my experiences in cooking in China as well as in Canada.

Introduction

Chinese cooking can easily be described as a type of cooking that has been perfected over the years through experimenting and improvising. Thus the cheapest source of raw material, the minimum amount of fuel and the maximum amount of preparation are the common practices. In my knowledge there are no written recipes in Chinese homes. The recipes are generally handed down from generation to generation and from neighbor to neighbor. Another reason for not having written recipes is that most of the women folk were illiterate in past generations. Since the turn of the twentieth century this illiteracy has started to change. Perhaps, in the future, there may be some uniformity in the ingredients used in the common dishes.

Some factors do definitely influence the choice of materials. For example, the lack of refrigeration leads to the use of freshly killed fowl or freshly picked vegetables, and the leftovers are usually preserved with highly concentrated salt solution, soy sauce or other spices. The preserving materials are a must in every meal preparation.

Soup is eaten as an individual and distinctive dish, and it is prepared and served with other dishes. The function of soup is somewhat similar to the glass of water served with a North American meal. Instead of taking a drink of water during the meal, the Chinese would take a drink of soup from the main soup dish, which is set in the middle of the table or at either end so that everyone can reach it. Most Chinese people do not seem to mind drinking the soup from the same bowl where everyone dips their spoon.

Meal Planning:

For generations it has been an accepted fact, by the Chinese, that their type of cooking, when eaten, will exert either a "hot air" effect or a "cold air" effect on the basic metabolism of man. In modern medicine one would perhaps explain such effects by the fact that certain foods will follow certain metabolic pathways and the metabolic rates can be determined. If the rates are fast, the Chinese call it a cold effect and if the rates are slow, the Chinese would call it a hot effect.

For the above reason, meal planning is extremely important in a Chinese home. A meal, then, must consist of a combination of these effects so that one would have a balanced sort of diet.

Briefly, I will attempt to list the types of foods which will belong to one of the following classifications, when cooked.

Classifications:
1. Cold air effect—all soups.
2. Hot air effect—all barbeuced meats and fried dishes that are cooked with an excess of oil or with hot spices.
3. Neutral effect (neither "hot" nor "cold")—all steamed dishes including those that use hot spices.

Such classification is not really adequate. This is just a broad classification. For a more detailed description one needs the great knowledge of a herbalist and I am not versed in this field. All my recipes are based upon the amounts normally consumed by four adults.

A typical Chinese meal could consist of:

1. Water cress soup
    Barbecued spareribs
    Beef and tomatoes
    Mushroom satin chicken
    Sliced chicken with peas-in-the-pod
    Rice
    Tea

One can substitute different dishes in the same categories to produce variations.

2. Here is a typical meal for a family who are weight conscious
    Winter melon soup
    Cod fish with bean sprouts ($\frac{1}{4}$ cup of fish)
    Steamed chicken with mushrooms ($\frac{1}{2}$ cup of chicken)
    Plain broccoli chop suey (no meat)
    Oyster sauce bean cakes
    Rice
    Tea

The only difference with meal number 2 in the cooking technique is that not as much oil is used as in the recipes. One teaspoon per dish may be the maximum amount used. The proportions of vegetables to meat is approximately 6 to 1.

Since I am not a dietician, the above information is based on the diets of myself and some very close friends. I must say that none of us weigh more than 130 pounds (whether male or female) which is a good weight for our heights.

House of Yee's Weekly Menu

Monday:
    Cantonese egg swirl soup
    Beef with buk choy (Chinese greens)
    Barbecued pork
    Steamed salted eggs with pork
    Rice
    Tea

Tuesday:
    Winter melon soup
    Steamed chicken with mushrooms
    Fried shrimp with Hoi sien jeung
    Fried cod fish with bean sprouts
    Rice
    Tea

Wednesday:
    Fresh lotus soup
    Fried squid with oyster sauce
    Steamed meat balls with salted turnips
    Shrimp fried hop choy (or swiss chard)
    Rice
    Tea

Thursday:
    Egg-flower swirl soup
    Oyster sauce bean curds (cakes)
    Garlic spareribs
    Satin spice chicken
    Rice
    Tea

Friday:
    Hairy melon soup
    Steamed Chinese sausage (4)
    Sliced chicken with peas-in-the-pod
    Black beans with Taro
    Rice
    Tea

Saturday:
    Mustard green soup
    Sweet and sour spareribs
    Mushroom satin chicken
    Aristocratic chop suey
    Rice
    Tea

Sunday:
> For lunch:
> Duck's feet congee or a big dish of fried rice or chow mein
> For supper:
> Mushroom bean curd soup
> Barbecued duck
> Beef and Tomatoes
> Fried cabbage with pork
> Rice
> Tea

If you are expecting guests, either invited or otherwise, all you need to do, for any of these menus, is to increase the amount of meat and vegetables in the above dishes as well as an increase of a half cup of rice for each additional person.

Economics:

Chinese cooking can cut your food bill down by as much as 50% or more, if you like rice. A pound of meat can be used for the preparation of 4-5 dishes. For example, a 3-4 lb. chicken can be made into one meat dish, one vegetable dish (with chicken) and the bones can be made into a soup. (See the recipes for the specific dishes) Some of the flavoring agents or Chinese ingredients may cost up to a dollar per jar or tin but a person only needs to replenish them a few times a year. For example, I have a tin of bean paste, (Saang See Jeung) which cost 60c, that was bought three months ago. I still have enough of this paste for many more meals. All Chinese salted ingredients keep for a very long time—six months to a year is quite a normal time for such things to last. It is true, of course, that if one buys the more exotic type of food such as eel maw ($7.50 a pound) or bird's nest soup (up to $10.00 a pound) that Chinese cooking may prove to be more expensive. The Chinese people only have such food at banquets or for special occasions, if at all.

Vegetables are an important part of a Chinese diet. Particularly in the summer months is the cost of a meal preparation most noticeable. One of my students told me in January that he had saved more than $20 per month since taking the course at night school. He also expects to double his savings in the summer months when vegetables are very inexpensive. There is no question about the economical advantages of Chinese cooking as well as the fact that the food is found to be so delicious by many people. I speak from personal experience in regards to the economical aspects for like many people I am budget conscious.

THE TECHNIQUES IN CHINESE COOKING

The techniques involved in Chinese cooking are: (a) frying, (b) steaming, (c) barbecuing, (d) deep frying, (e) prolonged cooking or "stewing", (f) a combination of the different methods.

Frying:

In general, the ingredients in any cooking, excluding pastries, are: 1. vegetable(s), 2. meat, 3. dehydrated or canned vegetable(s) or meat. A Chinese never overcooks his vegetables or meat, and he never boils his vegetables and strains the water before serving. Rather he slices his vegetables into bite-size pieces and fries them in a skillet with peanut oil. The peanut oil must be smoking before the vegetables are added. This smoking is the signal to start to put the vegetables into the skillet to fry. At the same time a little salt is sprinkled in the skillet and the vegetables are quickly and constantly mixed. The cook must always be ready to remove the skillet from the heat source if it gets too hot. This rarely happens once a person has attained skill in the technique of frying. After 1-2 minutes, the skillet will not show any signs of smoke due to the water content of the vegetables. If this is the case, there is no point in continuing the frying, for the vegetables are almost ready to serve. To be sure that they are evenly cooked, $\frac{1}{4}$-$\frac{1}{2}$ cup of water is added to the skillet and a lid is put on immediately for another two minutes. The heat should be on medium because the vegetables should not be allowed to burn on the bottom while they are not being mixed, and you do not want the water to disappear too fast. After two minutes the lid is removed. If there is still some water in the skillet, one teaspoon of cornstarch dissolved in $\frac{1}{3}$ cup of water is added in the middle of the skillet (with the vegetable pushed away from the centre) until the liquid has the consistency of gravy. All the starch solution may not be needed but the remaining amount can be used for another dish. Before the addition of the starch solution, you must make sure that the skillet is hot enough so that the cold starch mixture will be cooked seconds after it hits the skillet. That is, you may have to turn the heat to high to bring the water to boil before the starch solution is added. Now that's fine if there is some water in the skillet. What happens if the skillet is too dry or there is too much water? Well that's the time you should apply your common sense. If the vegetables are not cooked enough to suit your personal taste, you would add a little more water to continue the process, but if the vegetables are cooked just right, you would add a little water, bring it to a boil and then add the starch solution. If there is too much water, you can remove the lid and turn the heat to high. After 30 seconds a great deal of water would have evaporated and the starch solution can be added. You may wonder why one uses the starch solution at all. It is most important in Chinese cooking. The starch solution serves as a carrier or coagulating agent to coat all the bite-size pieces of vegetables with the natural flavor which may have been leeched, cooked or steamed out of the original vegetables. By the use of the starch solution, you do not lose anything from beginning to end in the cooking process, and the color of the vegetables should be appetizingly natural. The natural color will turn to yellow if the lid is taken off a few times to check the condition of your vegetables. Such a practice abhorred in Chinese cooking.

The preceding is the technique involved in cooking vegetables. Keeping this process in mind, it is conceivable that something else must be present to complete a dish. For this, spices and meat are used. That is why, in a given dish, there is often a name of the meat used plus the main vegetables. For example—chicken broccoli chop suey. Chop suey means a mixture of vegetables, usually celery, onions and bean sprouts. The next question is: How are the meats, spices and auxiliary vegetables cooked? The meat is cooked the same way as the vegetables. Heat peanut oil in a skillet until it starts to smoke, sprinkle a little salt in the skillet and add the meat, which has previously been sliced to the proper size. Then the meat is mixed for a minute or until it is cooked. For beef, mix it in the hot skillet for about 5 seconds and then remove it. Use the same skillet, which is still smoking, to cook the vegetables. With meat other than beef it is quite normal to leave it in the skillet while cooking the vegetables. In the case of beef, the meat is added again after the addition of the starch solution, mixed well and served.

The term vegetables applies to all the garden vegetables including dehydrated ones. The nature of different vegetables itself requires certain attention in the cooking process. Briefly we can classify vegetables into two categories: (1) those that can be eaten raw, (2) those that are not normally eaten raw. The first type, like celery and onions, is always used as a complementary vegetable. These vegetables will never consist of more than 20% of the vegetables used in a given dish. They may be called flavoring vegetables. Such things as tomatoes, peas-in-pods, bean sprouts, pea sprouts, and green peppers can be used either as complementary or main vegetables. Main vegetables, which consist of more than 50% of a given dish are those that are not usually eaten raw such as broccoli, cauliflower, swiss chard (hup choy), Chinese greens (buk choy), mustard greens, green beans, egg plant, spinach, asparagus, turnips, parsnips and cabbage. From the above classification it is quite logical that the "can be eaten raw" type of vegetable does not require much cooking while the second type requires more cooking than the first type.

Vegetables like Chinese radishes, cabbage, etc. are uniform in construction; that is they do not have stems and flower buds like broccoli or cauliflower. The former are usually cut into ¼ inch pieces as are the other complementary vegetables such as onions and celery. For broccoli, which has stems, it is quite understandable that the stems will take longer to cook than the rest of the broccoli plant. It is for this reason that the stems are sliced diagonally across into ¼ inch pieces.

An example of a dish using broccoli is beef broccoli chop suey. A brief outline of how this dish should be cooked is as follows:

(1a) Prepare a plate containing some sliced broccoli stems, broccoli flower buds, celery, onions and thinly sliced beef.

(1b) Heat a skillet containing 2 tablespoons of peanut oil until the oil smokes. Add a little salt.

(2) Fry the beef for about 5 seconds and remove the beef from the skillet.

(3) Place the stems of the broccoli in the skillet and cook about 20 seconds (it will look "bruised").

(4) Add the onion and celery and cook for about 10 seconds (until the smell of onion is apparent).

(5) Add the broccoli flower buds and leaves and cook about 30 seconds.

By now about a minute has elapsed since the process was started. Now is the time to add the spices. A Chinese cook would usually add 2 teaspoons of soy sauce and a ¼ of a teaspoon of monosodium glutamate. Mix constantly while adding the spices. As soon as the spices are added ½-¾ of a cup of water is poured into the skillet and the lid is immediately put on the skillet. The process of steaming is now in process and usually takes about two minutes. Do not remove the lid during this period. The cornstarch solution is now added and the beef is mixed with the vegetables just before the dish is served.

For meat dishes, such as garlic spareribs, chicken with green peppers or fried shrimp, the technique used is exactly the same as for meat used in vegetable dishes except the proportions are reversed eg. 50-80% meat and 50-20% of complementary vegetables. The meat is always cut into bite-size pieces rather than being sliced like the vegetables.

Let us look at a dish of chicken with green peppers. Chicken legs or breasts are most commonly used for this dish. The chicken is cut into bite-size pieces with the bones usually included in the pieces. The chicken should constitute 75% of the dish and the other 25% is green peppers (15%), onions (5%), and celery (5%).

The cooking procedure is as follows:

(1) Heat peanut oil in a skillet until it starts to smoke. Add some salt. Immediately add the chicken and mix constantly for 1-2 minutes.

(2) Push the chicken to the sides of the skillet and add the celery and onions. Stir for 30 seconds. Add the green peppers and mix with the celery and onions for another 30 seconds. Mix everything in the skillet together for 30 seconds.

(3) Add 1 tablespoon of soy sauce and mix once (about 10 seconds). Add a pinch of monosodium glutamate.

(4) Add ½-1 cup of water and cover with a lid immediately.

(5) Steam for 2-3 minutes.

(6) Add some cornstarch solution, mix and serve.

The foregoing discussions for vegetables and meat is that of frying and is used in almost every meal preparation in a Chinese home. The complementary vegetables such as bamboo shoots (canned), waterchestnuts (canned or fresh), dried mushrooms, dried cloud ears (a type of flavorful fungus like mushrooms), and golden needles (a type of dried lily flower) are often added if available. These are added in the cooking process right after the addition of celery and onions or before the steaming process. More information on these will be found in the following pages.

Common ingredients:

The common ingredients are used as flavoring agents. The use of a particular spice in large quantities produces a distinctive flavor whereas the use of the same spice in minute quantities produces an unrecognizable flavor. This is, perhaps, the secret of Chinese cooking and the spice used plus the amount depends upon the personal touch of the chef. For example, one chef may always add a trace amount of ginger, sesame seed oil or orange peel to all his dishes to produce his type of cooking, and another one may use the combination of the three or none at all. I, for example, always use a drop of sesame seed oil, if available. The only reason for this is the fact that I like this particular flavor.

These flavoring agents I will call complementary spices, because you do not have to have them, but to use them will enable you to produce a variety of dishes. The complementary spices are of either vegetable or meat origin. I shall classify them as complementary vegetables or meat.

1. Complementary vegetables:

a. Those which can always be obtained in fresh form from any super market such as celery, onions and green peppers.

b. Those which are exclusively supplied in Chinese grocery stores:

1. Waterchestnuts—fresh or canned. This is a crispy vegetable when raw or cooked. They have a texture like the "Delicious" apple but do not have the same flavor. The "Delicious" apple can be used as a substitute if waterchestnuts are not available but make sure not to overcook the apple, slice it very thin and add it to the other ingredients before serving.

2. Dried Chinese mushrooms—these are more flavorful than the common mushrooms.

3. Dried golden needles (lily flower).

4. Dried red dates—usually used in combination with golden needles.

5. Preserved turnips with or without a chili flavor.

6. Bean products—these all have an individual flavoring effect.

(a) dried black beans (dow see)—this is a strong flavoring agent.

(b) red bean paste (saang see jeung)—a semi-solid, milder flavoring agent.

(c) bean curd cake (naam yu)—this has a slightly fermented, cheesy flavor.

7. Dried cloud ears—a fungus, like mushrooms; also slightly crisp when cooked.

8. Chinese pickles—a mixture of ginger, carrots and green onion heads.

9. Preserved cucumbers.

10. Hoy sien jeung (sauce)—a mixture of bean paste and chili; hot, sweetish taste.

11. Plum sauce—greenish in color.

12. White nuts, lotus nuts and lily nuts—particularly used for soups.

2. Complementary meats:
1. Chinese sausage.
2. Soy sauce preserved pork, ducks and duck giblets.
3. Salted fish and eggs.
4. Shrimp paste—a strong cheese flavor.
5. Dried scallops, shrimps, lobster.
6. Dried oysters.
7. Oyster sauce.

Sauces:

In addition to the use of spices in the cooking of Chinese dishes, a number of sauces are always available. These sauces are placed on the table at each meal so that an individual can dip each morsel of food into the sauce of his liking to improve the delicacy of the food to his taste.

Plum sauce (Chinese green plums), English (dry) mustard, oyster sauce, a mixture of one part finely chopped ginger, peanut oil and soy sauce and a red pepper (a thick tabasco sauce) are commonly used for meat dishes.

Soy sauce and Chinese vinegar are used for fried noodles.

Substitution of Ingredients:

Many authentic Chinese dishes are not readily acceptable to Western tastes. These dishes have such a different flavor that one can only acquire a taste for them as one is willing to try the adventure involved in going through such an undertaking as to eat some of these dishes. Since this book is written with the use of genuine Chinese flavoring agents, there is a need to link these agents to the readily obtainable ingredients that are available in all supermarkets. The substitution used may not be as strong a flavoring agent as the genuine one and as a result the flavor obtained may be quite different, as should be expected. Nevertheless, cooking the Chinese way is more important, in my estimation, than the extensive use of flavoring agents or spices.

Chinese Ingredients:	Substituted by the following materials:
1. Waterchestnuts	Celery, raw "Delicious" apples for vegetable dishes
2. Oyster sauce	Soy sauce mixed with chicken concentrate or Ac'cent
3. Heung new fun (barbecue powder)	A mixture of one part of each of: star anise seeds, cinnamon powder, clove powder, dry ginger powder and powdered fennel, if available
4. Dow see (dried black beans)	3 parts soy sauce, 1 part garlic, 1 part ginger
5. Saang See Jeung (semi-solid red bean paste)	2 parts soy sauce, 1 part matured cheese. Mix these into a paste
6. Chinese Mushrooms	Canned or fresh mushrooms
7. Wun Zee (Cloud ears)	Canned or fresh mushrooms, thinly sliced
8. Bamboo shoots	Fresh parsnips, turnips or celery
9. Soy Sauce	Salt plus Ac'cent in beer
10. Bean Sprouts	Finely cut cabbage
11. Hoi saang jeung (sweetish chili bean paste)	1 part ketchup, 1 part ginger powder, 1 part garlic powder and 1 part chili
12. Golden needles	Fresh or canned mushrooms
13. Mei Jing, monosodium glutamate	Chicken concentrate, or Ac'cent
14. Rice Flour.	½ cornstarch and ½ all purpose flour

Fried Dishes

BEEF CHOP SUEY

¼ lb. lean beef, thinly sliced
½ cup sliced onions
½ cup sliced celery
2 cups bean sprouts (or substitute by thinly sliced cabbage)
salt and pepper

½ cup sliced mushrooms (fresh or Chinese)
2 tbsp. soy sauce
⅛ tsp. Ac'cent
1 tsp. cornstarch dissolved in ½ cup cool water
½ cup water

Heat two tbsp. of peanut oil in a skillet until it smokes. Add a little salt. Add the beef and stir quickly for 5 seconds; remove the beef immediately from the skillet. Add the vegetables in the above order stirring constantly after each addition (5-10 seconds). Add the soy sauce and Ac'cent and stir for another 10 seconds. Add ½ cup of water and immediately put a lid on the skillet. Leave for 2-3 minutes. Push the vegetables away from the center of the skillet and add the cornstarch solution slowly until the water thickens (like gravy). You may not need all the cornstarch solution. Add the beef again, mix and serve.

Additional vegetables can be added: bamboo shoots, broccoli, green peppers, waterchestnuts.

CHICKEN, PORK or SHRIMP CHOP SUEY

Use the same ingredients as for beef chop suey but substitute the beef by one of the individual meats above. Saute the meat for 1 minute before removing it from the skillet. For mushroom chop suey increase the amount of mushrooms to ¾ of a cup and omit the meat completely.

ARISTOCRATIC CHOP SUEY

½ cup squid

¼ cup onion

½ cup celery

1 clove garlic, finely chopped

1 tsp. fresh ginger, finely chopped

½ cup cloud ears

½ cup Chinese mushrooms

½ cup bamboo shoots

5 waterchestnuts

½ cup water

⅛ tsp. Ac'cent

1 tsp. cornstarch dissolved in ¼ cup of water

salt, pepper

2 tbsp. soy sauce

Soak the squid, cloud ears and Chinese mushrooms in separate containers 15-30 minutes before use. Slice the celery diagonally and the other vegetables about ¼ of an inch in width. Cut the squid according to the instruction on how to prepare squid for fried dishes on the following page. Heat the skillet with 2 tbsp. of peanut oil until it smokes. Sprinkle ⅛ tsp. of salt in the skillet, add the cut up squid and stir for 10 seconds or until the squid turns into cylindrical shapes. (Remember that the less you saute the squid the more tender it will be; the more the squid is sauted, the more leathery it will become). Remove the squid from the skillet, add the vegetables in the above order, stirring between each addition. After the last addition, the skillet should be cooled down a bit. Add 2 tbsp. soy sauce, ⅛ tsp. Ac'cent, salt and pepper, if needed. While mixing add ½-¾ cup of water. Immediately place a lid on the skillet for 2-3 minutes. Thicken the water, if any, with some of the cornstarch solution. Add the squid to the skillet, mix and serve.

HOW TO PREPARE SQUID FOR FRIED DISHES

Squid come in various forms—large, small and irregular, but they are all prepared the same way for frying. A large squid is usually about ¼" thick with a flat body, tentacles and a "backbone". The "backbone" is shaped like a shoe horn, is whitish in color and contains a high percentage of calcium. The first step in preparing the squid for use in a fried dish is to soak it for at least one hour. Then the backbone is removed by bending the squid at the end. The bone will become loose and can readily be peeled off. Any other hard, transparent coverings and any loose skin or membranes are then removed. The tentacles are cut into bite-size pieces. The body is now like a piece of thick leather. This is prepared in such a way, that when it is cooked, it should be tender and cylindrical in shape, like a small pine cone. This is done by spreading the squid in front of you, with the side where the backbone has been up. Hold a knife away from you at an angle of 30° and cut across the squid from one end to the other.

Cut 1/16" to $\frac{1}{8}$" in depth. Cut parallel lines to the first one about $\frac{1}{8}$" to $\frac{1}{4}$" apart. Now turn the squid about 45° and cut another set of parallel lines as above. Looking closely, you should now see a great number of little diamond shaped cuts over the entire squid. Now cut the squid into 2" squares. It is now ready for frying. With the sets of parallel lines, these 2" squares will form cylinders when they are heated, and the diamond shaped cuts will look like scales of a fish or like small pine cones.

BEEF WITH TOMATOES

$1\frac{1}{2}$ lbs. large tomatoes	1 clove garlic
$\frac{1}{4}$ cup onions	1 tbsp. vinegar (°)
$\frac{1}{4}$ cup celery	2 tbsp. sugar
$\frac{1}{4}$ lb. sliced beef steak or	1 tsp. cornstarch dissolved
rump roast	$\frac{1}{2}$ cup water
1 tbsp. soy sauce	salt, pepper

Place the tomatoes in a container and pour boiling water over them. Cover for $\frac{1}{2}$ minute. Replace the hot water with cool water and then peel the tomatoes. Cut each tomato into 6 wedges. Slice the onions and celery into $\frac{1}{4}$" pieces. Heat 2 tbsp. of peanut oil in a skillet until it smokes. Add a little salt. Add the sliced beef, saute for 5-10 seconds and remove the beef from the skillet. Add the onions, celery and garlic and mix for 30 seconds. Add the tomatoes, then the soy sauce, vinegar, sugar, salt and pepper. Cover with a lid for 2 minutes. Add the cornstarch solution until the water is thickened (like gravy). Add the beef, mix and serve.

(°) Add a little more vinegar if not sour enough, and a little more sugar if too sour.

TOMATO SAUCE

Use the above recipe, but cut the tomatoes, onions and celery very fine. It is also desirable to add some chopped green peppers and 1 tsp. of fresh ginger. This sauce can be used with Tomato Chicken, Tomato Cod-fish, Tomato Won Ton, Shrimp, Lobster or Crab.

PLAIN FRIED VEGETABLES

1 lb. broccoli

¼ cup onion

¼ cup celery

⅛ tsp. Ac'cent

2 tsp. soy sauce

1 tsp. cornstarch dissolved in water

¾ cup water

salt, pepper

Slice the stems of the broccoli diagonally into ⅛-¼ inch pieces and cut the flower buds into bite-size pieces. Also slice the celery and onion into ⅛-¼ inch pieces. Heat the skillet with 2 tbsp. of peanut oil until it smokes and add a little salt. Add the broccoli stems and saute for 30 seconds. Add the celery, onion and broccoli flower buds. Mix for another minute; add the soy sauce (you can add other bean paste products in addition to soy sauce or in place of soy sauce, if desired), Ac'cent, salt and pepper. Add ¾ cup of water, cover with a lid for 2 minutes. Use the cornstarch solution to thicken the water (so it is like gravy).

Cabbage, cauliflower, brussel sprouts, swiss chard, Chinese greens, mustard greens can be used in place of the broccoli.

TRANSLUCENT NOODLES

2 cups translucent noodles
  (fun see or see fun)

½ cup pork

¼ cup celery, chopped

¼ cup onions, chopped

2 Chinese mushrooms

1 tbsp. soy sauce

⅛ tsp. Ac'cent

1½ cup chicken broth

2 eggs

2 stalks green onions, chopped

pinch of pepper

Translucent noodles are factory produced and are bean products. They may be as long as two feet and have a "diameter" of a toothpick. The delicacy of this dish is that the "noodles" have a great absorbing power for other spices and flavors used with them.

Soak the noodles and mushrooms for 20 minutes. Drain the water off after this period of time. Slice the mushrooms. Heat 2 tbsp. of peanut oil in a skillet until it smokes. Add a little salt. Add the pork and stir for 30 seconds. Add the celery, onions, mushrooms and a little pepper. Stir for another 30 seconds. Add the noodles and turn the heat to low. Mix and add the chicken broth, soy sauce and Ac'cent. Mix and cover with a lid for 2 minutes. Add the two eggs and scramble with the noodles for 15 seconds. When the eggs start to set, remove the noodles to a serving dish and sprinkle the green onions on top before serving.

For variations: Substitute pork by shrimp, crab meat, or lobster. Remember not to overcook the eggs. This is important.

DICED ALMOND CHICKEN

½ cup blanched almonds, roasted and cut into quarters
½ lb. chicken breasts, diced
¼ cup onions, diced
¼ cup celery, diced
½ cup green peas, fresh or
frozen
½ cup bamboo shoots, diced

¼ cup mushrooms, fresh or Chinese
2 tbsp. soy sauce
⅛ tsp. Ac'cent
1 tsp. cornstarch dissolved in ½ cup
cold water
½ cup water
salt, pepper

Heat the skillet with 2 tbsp. of peanut oil until it smokes. Add a little salt. Add the breast of chicken which is cut into cubes. Saute the chicken for 1-2 minutes and remove from the skillet. Add onion, celery and other vegetables (except the almonds) in the above order while stirring. Stir for 1-2 minutes. Add soy sauce, Ac'cent, salt and pepper. Mix well and add ½ cup of water. Cover the skillet with a lid for a minute, then add the starch solution to thicken the water (like gravy). Add the almond and chicken cubes, mix well and serve.

SHRIMP WITH CHINESE RADISHES

1 lb. Chinese radishes
¼ lb. fresh, frozen shrimps
¼ cup celery
¼ cup onions
1 tbsp. pure soy sauce

1 tsp. cornstarch dissolved
in ½ cup cool water
1 tsp. finely chopped, fresh ginger
2 tsp. finely cut green onions
½ cup water

Clean the Chinese radishes like you would clean carrots. Cut the radishes finely with a coarse vegetable grater. Clean the shrimp (prawns) by removing the shells and legs. Make a slight incision length-wise along the back of the shrimp and remove the intestines. Sometimes the intestines are not visible unless there is some sand or sediment in them. Slice the shrimp into thin strips. Also slice the onions and celery.

Heat a skillet with 2 tbsp. of peanut oil until it smokes. Add a little salt. Add the shrimp and stir for 1 minute, then add the ginger and stir for another 5 seconds. Remove the shrimp and ginger from the skillet. Add the onions, celery and Chinese radishes; mix for one minute. Add the soy sauce while mixing, followed by ½ cup of water. Cover with a lid for 2-3 minutes (when the radishes are done they should not be crisp). Add enough of the starch solution to thicken the water (like gravy). Add the shrimp again and mix. Sprinkle the green onions on top before serving.

BLACK BEANS WITH TARO

1 lb. Chinese taro

$\frac{1}{4}$ lb. soy sauce preserved pork
   or fresh lean pork

$\frac{1}{4}$ cup onions

$\frac{1}{4}$ cup celery

2 tbsp. soy sauce

1 tsp. black beans, spice type

1 tsp. fresh ginger

1 tsp. garlic cloves

$\frac{1}{8}$ tsp. Ac'cent

$\frac{1}{2}$ cup water

2 tsp. chopped green onions

Chinese taro is somewhat like ordinary sweet potatoes. It is starchy, tender, not crispy, and grey in color when cooked. Clean the taro like you clean potatoes, cut it in halves and slice it into $\frac{1}{4}''$ pieces.

Using the blunt end of a knife, pound the black beans, ginger and garlic into a paste; add the soy sauce to this mixture (in a cup) and mix well. I will call this type of mixture of spices a "Universal Sauce".

Heat 2 tbsp. of peanut oil in a skillet until it smokes. Add a little salt. Add the sliced pork, saute until brown, and remove from the skillet. Add the onions, celery, and sliced taro and continue to mix for 1-2 minutes. Add Ac'cent, universal sauce and stir for another 30 seconds. Add $\frac{1}{2}$ cup of water and immediately cover the skillet with a lid for 3-4 minutes. Add the cooked pork and green onions, mix well and serve.

Turnips, parsnips, pumpkins and potatoes should be cooked the same way. By omitting the universal sauce, you would have the plain vegetable dish.

CODFISH WITH BEAN SPROUTS

$\frac{3}{4}$ lb. fillet of codfish

$\frac{3}{4}$ lb. bean sprouts

$\frac{1}{4}$ cup onions

$\frac{1}{4}$ cup celery

Ac'cent

$\frac{1}{2}$ tsp. garlic cloves

$\frac{1}{2}$ tsp. fresh ginger

1 tsp. soy sauce

1 tbsp. cornstarch dissolved in $\frac{1}{2}$
   cup of water

$\frac{1}{2}$ cup water

salt, pepper

Slice the fillet of codfish into $\frac{1}{8}$-$\frac{1}{4}$ inch pieces. Slice the onions and celery in a similar way. Crush the garlic and ginger and cut them finely.

Heat two tbsp. of peanut oil in a skillet until it smokes. Add a little salt. Add the sliced fish, mix for 5 seconds, add the ginger and garlic and mix for another 5-10 seconds. Remove the fish, garlic and ginger from the skillet. Add the celery, onions and bean sprouts. Mix for 1 minute. Add Ac'cent, soy sauce, ½ cup of water, salt and pepper. Cover with a lid for 1 minute. Add the cornstarch solution until the water is thickened (like gravy). Remove the vegetables from the skillet with a slotted spoon and spread them on a platter. Put the fish back in the skillet so it can be "coated" with the "gravy" from the vegetables. Remove the fish and spread it on top of the vegetables. Sprinkle a generous amount of pepper on the fish before serving.

Substitute codfish by lingcod, bass, pickrel, or whitefish.

OYSTER SAUCE BEAN (Cake) CURD (°)

3 bean curd cakes	4 tbsp. of oyster sauce
3 green onions	Salt, pepper
¼ cup onions	¼ cup water
1 clove of garlic, chopped	

Bean (cake) curds can be bought fresh from Chinatown. They are white, 4" x 4" x 1" in size and are usually displayed, by the front window of the store, submerged in a tub of water. Each cake should be cut into 6 pieces before use.

Heat 2 tbsp. of peanut oil in a skillet on low heat. Add a little salt. Add the bean cakes in one layer and stir them every 30 seconds until they are slightly brown. Turn heat to high, push the bean cakes aside and add the onions, green onions, which are cut in 1½" lengths, and the garlic. Mix for 30 seconds. Remove the skillet from the heat and after 30 seconds add the oyster sauce and mix well (if the skillet is too hot the oyster sauce will burn). Add ¼ cup of water, cover with a lid for 1-2 minutes under low heat. Sprinkle some chopped green onions on top before serving, if desired.

(°) Vitamin Content: Calculated on a dry basis per 100 grams of bean curd. Vitamin A—110 IU, Thiamine—1.14 mg., Riboflavin—0.31 mg., Niacin—2.1 mg.

Amino Acids: Glutamic Acid 7.2%, Leucine 3.2%, Arginine 3.0%, Lysine 2.6 per cent, Valine 2.0 per cent, Isoleucine 2.0 per cent, Phenylalanine 2.0 per cent, Threonine 1.6 per cent, Histidine 0.9 per cent, Tryptophane 0.64 per cent, Methionine 0.56 per cent.

Calories: 350 cal./100 gm.

SLICED CHICKEN WITH PEAS-IN-THE-POD

¼ cup thinly sliced breast of chicken

¾ lb. peas-in-the-pod

½ cup onions

¼ cup celery

1 tsp. black beans

1 tbsp. soy sauce

⅛ tsp. Ac'cent

1 tsp. cornstarch dissolved in ½ cup of water

⅓ cup water

Salt, pepper

Clean the peas-in-the-pod, which are ordinary garden peas which are picked when they are very young so that the pods can be eaten as well, by cutting off a small amount of either end (do not attempt to remove the young peas) and rinse well with water.

Heat 2 tbsp. of peanut oil in a skillet until it smokes. Add a little salt. Add the sliced chicken, saute for 30 seconds to 1 minute and remove from the skillet. Add the celery, onions and peas-in-the-pod and mix for another minute. Add the soy sauce and the black beans which have previously been pounded into a paste with 1 tbsp. of soy sauce (this is in addition to the soy sauce in the list of ingredients). Mix for 30 seconds, add ⅓ cup of water and cover with a lid for 1-2 minutes. Add enough of the cornstarch solution to thicken the water (like gravy). Return the chicken to the skillet, mix and serve.

This dish can be turned into a meat dish by increasing the amount of chicken to ¾ of a pound and decreasing the peas-in-the-pod to ¼ pound.

CURRIED CHICKEN

1-2½ lbs. fryer chicken

4 tbsp. curry powder

¼ cup tomatoes, finely cut

1 cup onions

½ cup celery

1 tsp. cornstarch dissolved in 1 cup of water

½ tsp. vinegar

1 tsp. sugar

½ tsp. pepper

2 tbsp. soy sauce

⅛ tsp. Ac'cent

1 cup water

Cut the chicken into bite-size pieces (include the bones). Heat 2 tbsp. of peanut oil in a skillet until it smokes. Add a little salt. Add chicken and saute for 1 minute. Add celery, and onions and stir for 1 minute. While mixing add tomatoes, pepper, soy sauce and Ac'cent. Add 1 cup of water and then the curry, vinegar and sugar. Cover with a lid and simmer for at least 10 minutes. Skim any excess fat off the top. Add enough of the starch solution to thicken the water like gravy). Serve.

Although this dish is done after 10 minutes, the curry will have a sharp taste. The curry will taste smooth and mild if it is simmered up to ½ hour. If this is done, an additional ¾ cup of water must be added to allow for evaporation.

For other curry dishes substitute chicken by beef, spareribs, duck, shrimps, fresh oysters, lobster or crab. With lobster or crab, be sure to clean before using and cut into bite-size pieces, leave the shells on. If you like hot curry, add ½ tsp. chili powder.

SWEET AND SOUR SPARERIBS

1 lb. pork spareribs, cut into 1" pieces

¼ cup celery

½ cup cucumbers

¼ cup vinegar

3 tbsp. sugar

½ cup tomatoes

1 cup lettuce

1 clove garlic, crushed

1 tsp. barbecue powder (Heung new fun)

1 egg

½ cup cornstarch

1 tsp. cornstarch dissolved in ½ cup of water

1 cup water

½ tsp. salt, ⅛ tsp. pepper

1 tbsp. soy sauce

Place the spareribs in a bowl and add 1 tbsp. soy sauce, salt, pepper, 1 egg, 1 tbsp. sugar, 1 tbsp. vinegar, 1 tsp. barbecue powder, and ½ cup cornstarch. Mix well until the spareribs are covered with this mixture (or batter).

Heat ½ cup of peanut oil in a skillet until it smokes. Add a little salt. Add the spareribs and stir occasionally to prevent burning on the bottom. After 10 minutes, the spareribs will be golden brown. Drain the excess oil from the skillet. Add the finely cut garlic and mix for 10 seconds. Add 1 cup of water, ¼ cup of vinegar, 2 tbsp. of sugar and enough of the starch solution to thicken the mixture. Simmer for 15-20 minutes.

Before preparing the spareribs, cut the cucumbers into quarters and slice diagonally. Slice the tomatoes, lettuce and celery; add 3 tbsp. vinegar, 1½ tbsp, sugar and ¼ tsp. of salt. Mix well and let marinate for at least 20 minutes (mix occasionally). After 20 minutes, drain the vegetables and place on a serving dish. Place the spareribs on top of the vegetables before serving.

Sweet and Sour pork, chicken, chicken liver and pig's feet are made the same way as sweet and sour spareribs by substituting the appropriate meat. With pig's feet, simmer for at least 3 hours.

Pineapple spareribs, lichee nut spareribs, dragon eyes spareribs and Chinese pickles spareribs are made similarly by adding the proper fruit to the sweet and sour spareribs before serving.

FRIED PEAS WITH EGGS

4 eggs

½ cup onions, chopped

¼ cup celery, sliced

1 cup frozen peas

¼ cup minced pork or chicken

¼ cup finely cut fresh tomatoes

Salt, pepper

Heat 2 tbsp. of peanut oil in a skillet until it smokes. Add a little salt. Add the pork or chicken and saute for 1 minute. Add the sliced celery and onions and stir for 30 seconds. Add the peas (unfrozen) and stir for 1 minute. Add a little salt and pepper. Turn the heat to low and add the eggs. Scramble the eggs with the vegetables for 15-20 seconds. Remove the mixture to a serving dish. The cooking process will continue by its own heat while on the dish. Sprinkle the finely cut tomatoes on top to give a good contrasting color effect.

MUSHROOM VELVET CHICKEN

1 cup Chinese mushrooms
or canned, fresh mushrooms

¾ lb. chicken breasts

½ cup celery

¼ cup onions

1 tsp. fresh ginger, chopped

2 tsp. soy sauce

1 tsp. peanut oil

⅛ tsp. Ac'cent

1 tsp. cornstarch dissolved in ½ cup water

2 drops sesame seed oil

Salt, pepper

¼ cup water

1 tsp. cornstarch (dry)

Slice the chicken extremely thin and marinate it at least 10 minutes with a little salt, pepper, 1 tsp. soy sauce, 1 tsp. cornstarch, 1 tsp. peanut oil, 2 drops of sesame seed oil and ⅛ tsp. Ac'cent. Soak the Chinese mushrooms at least one half hour before use.

Heat 2 tbsp. peanut oil in a skillet until it smokes. Add a little salt. Add celery and onions and mix for 30 seconds. Add the sliced mushrooms and ¼ cup of water and cover with a lid for 30 seconds. Add enough of the starch solution to thicken the water (like gravy). Remove from the skillet. Rinse the skillet and heat until dry. Add 1 tbsp. of peanut oil and heat the skillet until the oil smokes. Add a little salt. Add the chicken and mix for 30 seconds, then add the ginger and stir for 5 seconds. Add the cooked vegetables; mix well for another 30 seconds and serve.

Note: Overcooking the chicken is not acceptable in this dish—BE CAREFUL!

GOLDEN NEEDLES, RED DATES, BRAISED CHICKEN

5-10 Chinese red dates
$\frac{1}{8}$ cup dried golden needles
5 Chinese mushrooms
2 cloves garlic
$\frac{3}{4}$ lb. chicken legs, breasts or thighs
$\frac{1}{4}$ cup onions
Salt, pepper

$\frac{1}{4}$ cup celery
1 tsp. fresh ginger, chopped
2 tsp. soy sauce
$\frac{1}{8}$ tsp. Ac'cent
1 tsp. cornstarch dissolved in $\frac{1}{2}$ cup water
$\frac{1}{2}$ tsp. sugar
$\frac{3}{4}$ cup water

Chop the chicken into bite-size pieces including the bones. Soak the red dates, golden needles and Chinese mushrooms $\frac{1}{2}$ hour before use. Cut the golden needles in halves; slice the mushrooms and red dates, removing the stones in the red dates while slicing.

Place the chicken in a bowl and mix well with chopped garlic, ginger, Ac'cent, salt and pepper, and sugar. Let stand at least 15 minutes.

Heat 2 tbsp. of peanut oil in a skillet until it smokes. Add a little salt. Saute chicken until slightly brown (about 1 minute). Add celery, onions and soaked vegetables. Mix for $\frac{1}{2}$ minute, add $\frac{3}{4}$ cup of water and cover with a lid. Simmer for 10-15 minutes. Remove all the vegetables from the skillet with a slotted spoon and place on a serving dish. Place the chicken on top of the vegetables. Thicken the water in the skillet with enough of the cornstarch solution to make a "gravy". Pour this on top of the chicken before serving.

DRIED SPARERIBS WITH GARLIC

1 lb. spareribs
2 tbsp. finely chopped garlic
1 tbsp. soy sauce
$\frac{1}{2}$ tsp. sugar

1 cup lettuce
2 tbsp. cornstarch
$\frac{1}{8}$ tsp. Ac'cent
Salt, pepper

Place the spareribs in a bowl, after cutting them into 1" x $\frac{1}{2}$" pieces. Add a little salt, pepper, the soy sauce, sugar, cornstarch and Ac'cent. Mix well and marinate for at least 15 minutes.

Heat 2 tbsp. peanut oil in a skillet until it smokes. Add a little salt. Add the spareribs, mix occasionally (every 30 seconds) until the spareribs are golden brown. Turn the heat down to low and cover with a lid for 2-3 minutes. Remove the excess oil and fat and increase the heat to high. While mixing, add the finely chopped garlic. Mix well for 30 seconds or until the garlic is brown and nicely coated over the spareribs. Transfer the spareribs to a serving platter and use the finely cut lettuce to form a ring around the spareribs.

RED BEAN PASTE SPARERIBS

1 lb. spareribs
¼ cup celery
¼ cup onions
2 tbsp. red bean paste
  (saang see jeung)
1 tsp. fresh garlic
1 tsp. cornstarch

1 tsp. soy sauce
½ tsp. sugar
1 tsp. cornstarch dissolved in ½ cup
  water
⅛ tsp. Ac'cent
1 small tomato
½ cup water

Cut the spareribs into 1" x ½" pieces. Marinate the spareribs with salt, pepper, ½ tsp. soy sauce, ½ tsp. sugar, and 1 tsp. cornstarch, for 10 minutes.

Heat 2 tbsp. peanut oil in a skillet until it smokes. Add a little salt. Add the spareribs and stir for 1-2 minutes or until they are golden brown. Drain the excess fat. Add the garlic and stir for 10 seconds; add the celery, and onions and mix for another 30 seconds. Add ½ tsp. soy sauce, 2 tbsp. red bean paste and ⅛ tsp. Ac'cent and mix for another 10 seconds. Add ½ cup of water, cover with a lid and simmer for 15 minutes. Thicken the water with enough of the cornstarch solution to make a "gravy". Transfer to a serving plate. Slice the tomato as thinly as possible and use it to form a ring around the spareribs.

Black beans (dow see), universal sauce or oyster sauce can be used in place of the red bean paste for variations.

CANTONESE LOBSTER

1 live lobster
¼ lb. Chinese preserved pork
  or loin pork
2 tbsp. black beans (dow see)
1 tsp. fresh ginger
1 tsp garlic clove
2 tsp. soy sauce

1 tsp. sugar
1 tbsp. cornstarch
⅛ tsp. Ac'cent
¼ cup onions
2 eggs
1 cup water
Salt, pepper

Clean the lobster as in the recipe for Oyster Sauce Lobster. Slice the pork very thin and mix with a little salt and pepper, ⅛ tsp. sugar, 1 tsp. soy sauce and ½ tsp. cornstarch and let stand for 10 minutes.

Heat 2 tbsp. of peanut oil in a skillet until it smokes. Add a little salt. Add the pork and mix for 10 seconds, then add the lobster and mix for another 10 seconds. Add onions, universal sauce (made by crushing the black beans, garlic, and ginger together and mixing with the soy sauce), ½ tsp. sugar, Ac'cent, and a little salt and pepper. Mix for 10 seconds and add 1 cup of water. Cover with a lid and simmer for 10 minutes. Use the rest of the cornstarch dissolved in ⅛ cup of water and stir enough of this solution into the lobster mixture until it thickens like gravy. Remove the skillet from the heat and mix two beaten eggs into the lobster mixture. It is very important to remove the skillet from the heat before adding the eggs. If added while the skillet is on the heat, the dish is not acceptable!

OYSTER SAUCE LOBSTER

1 live large lobster
½ cup pork
¼ cup celery
1 tsp. ginger, chopped
1 tsp. fresh garlic, chopped
1 tsp. sugar
3 tbsp. oyster sauce

1 tsp. soy sauce
1 tsp. cornstarch dissolved in ½ cup water
⅛ tsp. Ac'cent
½ cup water
Pepper

Slice the pork very thin (it is more suitable if you can find some fat on the pork such as pork used to make bacon). Cut off the lobster's claws and legs. Split the lobster lengthwise and remove the stomach, intestines, etc. Cut the lobster meat into bite-size pieces with the shell on.

Heat 2 tbsp. peanut oil in a skillet until it smokes. Add a little salt. Add the pork and stir for 10 seconds. Add the lobster and stir for 30 seconds. Add the ginger and garlic and stir for 10 seconds, then add the celery and stir for 10 seconds. Add the soy sauce, sugar, Ac'cent, and a little pepper. Turn the heat to low and add 3 tbsp. oyster sauce. Mix well and immediately add ½ cup of water. Simmer for 5-10 minutes. Add enough of the starch solution to thicken the water like gravy. Never use canned lobster.

Fresh shrimp or crabs can be used as substitutes for the lobster to produce variations.

OYSTER SAUCE ABALONE

1 can abalone
½ cup abalone water
¼ cup oyster sauce
1 tsp. soy sauce

1 tsp. garlic clove
¼ cup onions
1 tsp. cornstarch dissolved in ½ cup abalone water

Cut and cook the onions, garlic and abalone as in the recipe for Cantonese Abalone. After 10 seconds, turn the heat down and add the oyster sauce, soy sauce and abalone water. Thicken with the cornstarch solution (made with abalone water).

CANTONESE ABALONE

$\frac{3}{4}$ lb. canned abalone
$\frac{1}{4}$ cup onions
$\frac{1}{4}$ cup celery
4 Chinese mushrooms
$\frac{1}{2}$ cup bamboo shoots
5 waterchestnuts
1 tsp. fresh garlic
1 tsp. fresh ginger

1 tsp. sugar
1 tbsp. soy sauce
1 tsp. cornstarch dissolved in $\frac{1}{2}$ cup
   water
$\frac{1}{2}$ cup water
$\frac{1}{8}$ tsp. Ac'cent
Salt, pepper

Slice the abalone about $\frac{1}{8}''$-$\frac{1}{4}''$ in thickness. Slices all the other ingredients into thin pieces. Chinese mushrooms must be soaked for $\frac{1}{2}$ hour before use. The fresh waterchestnuts must be peeled and washed before being sliced.

Heat 2 tbsp. of peanut oil in a skillet until it smokes. Add a little salt. Add the sliced onions, celery, bamboo shoots, waterchestnuts and mushrooms and stir for 30 seconds. Add $\frac{1}{2}$ cup of water; cover with a lid and simmer for 3 minutes. Remove the vegetables from the skillet. Heat the skillet again until dry and add 1 tbsp. of peanut oil. Heat until it smokes. Add the garlic, ginger and abalone and mix for 10 seconds. Add the cooked vegetables, soy sauce, sugar and a little pepper. Immediately thicken with enough of the cornstarch solution to make a gravy. Remember that overcooking the abalone will make it leathery if fresh abalone is used.

TOMATO SHRIMP BALLS

1 lb. fresh frozen shrimp
$\frac{1}{4}$ cup celery
$\frac{1}{4}$ cup onions
1 tsp. garlic clove
4 tsp. sugar
$\frac{1}{4}$ cup cornstarch
1 cup green peppers

5 Chinese mushrooms
4 medium size tomatoes
1 tsp. pepper, 1 tsp. salt
1 cup water
2 tbsp. soy sauce
Peanut oil

Remove the shells from the shrimp; slice the shrimp lengthwise through the back and remove the intestinal track, if any. Mince the shrimp and add 2 tbsp. cornstarch, 1 tsp. pepper, 1 tsp. salt, 1 tsp.

sugar, 1 tbsp. soy sauce and 1 tsp. peanut oil. Stir the mixture until well blended. Scald the tomatoes, peel and reduce to a pulp. Slice the other vegetables to small pieces.

Prepare a pot of boiling water. Scoop a teaspoon of the shrimp mixture from the bowl and form it into balls (as round as possible). Drop each ball into the boiling water and cook until the ball floats to the top of the water. Remove the shrimp balls from the water to a bowl.

Heat two tbsp. of peanut oil in a skillet until it smokes. Add a little salt. Add the celery, green peppers, mushrooms, onions, garlic and a little pepper. Mix for 1 minute and add the cooked shrimp balls. Mix for 30 seconds. Add the tomato pulp, 1 tbsp. soy sauce, 1 tsp. sugar and $\frac{1}{2}$ cup of water. Mix. Cover with a lid for 2 minutes. Add enough of the cornstarch solution to thicken the water (like gravy). Serve.

FRIED SHRIMP WITH SHELLS

1 lb. fresh frozen shrimp
1 tbsp. vinegar
1 tsp. sugar
$\frac{1}{4}$ cup celery, sliced
$\frac{1}{4}$ cup onions, sliced
Salt, pepper
1 tsp. ginger (fresh), chopped

1 tsp. garlic cloves, chopped
3 tbsp. hoi sien jeung (sauce) (°)
1 tsp. soy sauce
1 tsp. cornstarch dissolved in $\frac{1}{2}$ cup of water
$\frac{1}{2}$ cup of water

Make a slight incision in the back of each unfrozen shrimp by cutting through the shells lengthwise. Remove the intestines, pull off the legs, wash, drain and place on a paper towel.

Heat 2 tbsp. of peanut oil in a skillet until it smokes. Add a little salt. Fry the shrimp 30 seconds on each side. Add the celery, onions, garlic, ginger, salt and pepper. While mixing, add the hoi sien jeung, sugar, vinegar, soy sauce, and $\frac{1}{2}$ cup water. Simmer for 1-2 minutes with a lid on the skillet. Thicken the contents of the skillet if necessary with enough of the starch solution to make a gravy.

(°) Chili bean paste.
The hoi sien jeung (Chili bean paste) may be substituted by Black beans (dow see) or other type of bean products.

BEEF GLUTEN

½ tsp. sugar
1 tbsp. soy sauce
1 tsp. cornstarch dissolved in ½ cup water
Water
Salt, pepper

3 lb. flour, all purpose
½ lb beef tenderloin or New York cut
¼ cup celery
1 tsp. fresh ginger
2 tbsp. oyster sauce

Place the flour in a bowl, add water gradually and mix until it appears like bread dough. Let sit for 1 hour. Add water to cover dough and knead. Remove the water. Continue adding water, kneading and removing the water until the water is relatively clear. This removes most of the starch. The procedure should be repeated 5-10 times. Squeeze the resulting gluten hard to remove most of the water. Cut the gluten into 1" x ½" x ½" pieces and coat each piece with dry all purpose flour.

Heat 2 tbsp. of peanut oil in a skillet until it smokes. Add a little salt. Add ginger and immediately add the beef, which has been sliced into 1"x ¼" pieces. Saute for 10-15 seconds and remove from the skillet. Add celery and gluten pieces and mix for 1-2 minutes. Turn heat to low and add the soy sauce, oyster sauce, sugar, ½ cup water, salt and pepper. Simmer for 5 minutes. Thicken with enough of the cornstarch solution to make a gravy. Add beef again, mix and serve.

GINGER BEEF

1 lb. New York cut steak or sirloin steak
1 cup onions, sliced
1 tsp. garlic cloves
1 tbsp. fresh ginger
1 tsp. cornstarch
½ cup water

½ cup cashew nuts (or peanuts or almonds)
1 tbsp. lemon juice
1 tsp. sugar
1 tbsp. soy sauce
⅛ tsp. Ac'cent

Cut the beef into 1" x ½" x ¼" pieces. Chop the ginger and garlic very finely. Mix the cornstarch, soy sauce, Ac'cent, sugar, and lemon into the ½ cup of water. Chop the cashew nuts as finely as possible.

Heat 2 tbsp. of peanut oil in a skillet until it smokes. Add a little salt. Add onions and mix for 5 seconds. Push the onions to one side, add the ginger and garlic and mix for 5 seconds. Add the beef and stir it quickly for 25-30 seconds. Immediately add the above sauce mixture and stir well for another 5 seconds or until the mixture thickens. Remove and serve after sprinkling nuts on top.

BEEF WITH OYSTER SAUCE

¾ lb. beef (tenderloin, New
  York cut)
½ cup celery
½ tsp. sugar
2 tbsp. oyster sauce

½ cup chicken broth or
1 tbsp. chicken concentrate in ½
  cup water
1 tsp. cornstarch
Salt, pepper

Slice the celery diagonally into ¼" pieces. Slice the beef (across the grain) into 1" x ½ x ¼" pieces.

Heat 2 tbsp. of peanut oil in a skillet until it smokes. Add a little salt. Add celery and mix for 15 seconds. Add the beef and saute for another 15 seconds. Turn heat to low. Add a sauce made by mixing the ½ cup of chicken broth, ½ tsp. sugar, 2 tbsp. of oyster sauce and 1 tsp. of cornstarch. Mix and immediately place on a serving dish. This dish should be made in about 1 minute. If medium cooked beef is objectionable, simmer for another minute before serving.

BEAN CURD FISH

1 3 to 5 lb. fish (cod, bass,
  or salmon)
½ tsp. garlic clove
1 tsp. fresh ginger
2 tbsp. oyster sauce
3 stalks of green onions
2 tsp. cornstarch dissolved in
  ⅓ cup water

2 tbsp. soy sauce
¼ tsp. pepper
2 cakes bean curd
⅛ tsp. Ac'cent or
2 tsp. chicken concentrate in 1 cup
  water
1 tsp. sugar
Water

Clean the fish by removing the scales, intestines and head if desired. Chop the ginger and garlic finely. Mix the soy sauce, oyster sauce, pepper, sugar and Ac'cent (or chicken concentrate) in ½ cup of water. Cut the green onions into 2" lengths, including the green part. Cut each bean curd into 6 pieces.

Heat 2 tbsp. of peanut oil in a skillet on low heat. Add the fish and brown on each side for 2 minutes. Add the garlic, ginger and green onions to the skillet and mix for 5-10 seconds. Add the above sauce mixture followed by enough water to barely cover the fish. Cover the skillet with a lid and simmer for 10-15 minutes or until done. Remove the fish carefully to a serving dish. Add the bean curds to the skillet and turn the heat to high to evaporate some of the water (leave the lid off). After 2-3 minutes, add enough of the starch solution to thicken the water to a gravy like consistency. Pour the hot sauce over the fish. Arrange the bean curds around the fish.

ALMOND FISH CAKES

$\frac{1}{2}$ lb. fresh, frozen shrimp
$\frac{1}{2}$ lb. fillet of cod or pickerel
$\frac{1}{2}$ cup green onions
1 tsp. fresh ginger
3 tbsp. peanut oil
$\frac{1}{4}$ cup blanched almonds
1 tbsp. soy sauce

1 tbsp. cornstarch
$\frac{1}{2}$ tsp. salt
$\frac{1}{4}$ tsp. pepper
$\frac{1}{2}$ cup chicken broth or
1 tbsp. chicken concentrate in $\frac{1}{2}$ cup water

Remove the shells from the shrimp; slice the shrimp lengthwise through the back and remove the intestinal track, if any. Chop the shrimp, fish meat, almonds, green onions and ginger together until it looks like hamburger. Place this mixture in a bowl and add the salt, pepper, soy sauce, 1 tbsp. peanut oil and the cornstarch. Blend well. Shape mixture into 8-10 patties.

Heat the skillet with 2 tbsp, peanut oil under low heat. Add the patties separately to the skillet and fry for 1-2 minutes on each side. (until golden brown). Remove the patties to a serving plate.

Add the chicken broth to the skillet. When it boils, stir in enough cornstarch solution (made from 1 tsp. cornstarch dissolved in $\frac{1}{2}$ cup of water) to thicken the solution. Pour this "gravy" over the fish patties before serving.

Ginger powder can be used as a substitute for the fresh ginger.

STUFFED FISH

1 3-5 lb. large bone fish
5 Chinese mushrooms
5 waterchestnuts
1 tsp. garlic cloves
1 tsp. sugar
1 tsp. cornstarch
4 tbsp. peanut oil

1 tbsp. soy sauce
1 tsp. fresh ginger
$\frac{1}{2}$ cup of chicken broth or
2 tbsp. chicken concentrate in $\frac{1}{2}$ cup water
Salt, pepper
$\frac{1}{2}$ cup onions

Remove the scales, head and intestines from the fish and wash. One can use cod, carp, bass or pickerel. Soak the mushrooms at least 15 minutes before use and slice them after the soaking period. Peel, wash and slice the waterchestnuts. Slice the onions and chop the ginger and garlic very finely.

Heat 2 tbsp. of peanut oil in a skillet until it smokes. Add a little salt. Add the onions, garlic and ginger and mix for 10-20 seconds. Add the mushrooms and waterchestnuts and mix for another 10-20 seconds. Mix the chicken broth with the soy sauce, sugar 1 tsp. of cornstarch, salt, and pepper. Add this sauce to the skillet. Remove everything from the skillet. Rinse skillet. Heat 2 tbsp. of peanut oil in the skillet on medium heat (not until it smokes). Add the fish and braise on 1 side for 5 minutes with a lid on the skillet. Turn the fish over and braise on the other side for 5 minutes. Spread the cooked vegetables on top and around the fish and braise for another 5 minutes. Place fish on a serving plate and spread any remaining vegetables over the fish.

If there is not enough gravy-like sauce remaining, add a little water, for this dish requires this type of sauce.

SWEET AND SOUR FISH

1 3-4 lb. fish (carp, bass, cod)	3 tbsp. sugar
$\frac{1}{2}$ cup onions	1 cup cucumbers or Chinese sweet pickles
$\frac{1}{2}$ cup celery	
1 tsp. fresh ginger	1 tsp. cornstarch dissolved in $\frac{1}{2}$ cup water
1 tsp. garlic cloves	
1 tbsp. chili bean paste (hoi sien jeung)	$1\frac{1}{2}$ cups water
	Salt, pepper
$\frac{1}{4}$ cup vinegar	4 tbsp. peanut oil

Clean the fish by removing scales, head and intestines if desired. Rub a little salt on the fish. Slice the onions, celery, and cucumbers and chop the ginger and garlic very finely.

Heat skillet under low heat with 2 tbsp. of peanut oil. Place the fish on one side in the skillet and fry for 5 minutes. Turn the fish over and fry for another 5 minutes. During this last five minutes heat another skillet with another 2 tbsp. of peanut oil until it smokes. Add a little salt. Add the garlic, and ginger and mix for 5 seconds. Add the celery, onions and cucumbers and mix for 10 seconds. Add $1\frac{1}{2}$ cups of water, then add the sugar, vinegar and chili bean paste. Mix. Thicken the mixture with enough of the cornstarch solution to make a gravy. Pour this sweet and sour sauce over the fish and simmer for 5 minutes. Serve.

PINEAPPLE CHICKEN BALLS

1 2 to 3 lb. fryer
1-15 oz. tin pineapple cubes
  including the juice
2 eggs
1 tsp. soy sauce
$\frac{1}{2}$ cup water
$\frac{1}{8}$ cup flour

$\frac{2}{3}$ cup cornstarch
1 tbsp. baking powder
3 tbsp. sugar
2 tbsp. cornstarch dissolved in $\frac{1}{4}$
  cup water
Salt, pepper

Remove the bones from the chicken and cut it into bite-size pieces. Mix the chicken with 1 tsp. soy sauce and a little salt and pepper. Prepare a batter by mixing 2 eggs, $\frac{1}{8}$ cup of flour, $\frac{2}{3}$ cup of cornstarch, $\frac{1}{2}$ cup of water and 1 tbsp. of baking powder. Dip individual pieces of chicken into this batter and then drop them into a deep fryer at 375-400°F for 2 minutes. When the chicken is golden brown, remove from the fryer and place on paper towels to drain the excess oil. In the meantime, prepare the pineapple sauce by mixing the pineapple juice, the pineapple cubes and sugar in a sauce pan. When the mixture boils, stir in the cornstarch solution to thicken. Mix the chicken with this sauce seconds before serving.

Lichee nuts or dragon's eyes can be substituted for the pineapple to obtain Lichee nut or dragon's eyes chicken balls.

MUSHROOM CHICKEN BALLS

2-3 lb. fryer
$\frac{1}{2}$ cup celery
$\frac{1}{2}$ cup bamboo shoots
8 waterchestnuts
5 Chinese mushrooms or
1 cup canned mushrooms
1 tsp. fresh garlic, chopped
1 egg

$\frac{1}{2}$ cup water
1 tbsp. baking powder
$\frac{1}{8}$ cup all purpose flour
$\frac{2}{3}$ cup cornstarch
1 tbsp. soy sauce
1 cup chicken broth
1 tbsp. cornstarch dissolved in $\frac{1}{8}$
  cup water

Remove the bones from the fryer and cut it into bite-size pieces. Mix the chicken with a little salt and pepper. Prepare a batter by mixing 1 egg, $\frac{1}{2}$ cup water, 1 tbsp. baking powder, $\frac{1}{8}$ cup of flour and $\frac{2}{3}$ cup of cornstarch. Coat the chicken with the batter. Drop individual pieces into a deep fryer for 2 minutes (until golden brown). Strain from the oil.

Soak the Chinese mushrooms for at least 20 minutes before use. Cut the celery, bamboo shoots, waterchestnuts (which have been peeled and washed) and mushrooms into thin, small pieces.

Heat two tbsp. peanut oil in a skillet until it smokes. Add a little salt. Add the celery and garlic and stir for 10 seconds. Add the bamboo shoots, waterchestnuts, and mushrooms and stir for 30 seconds. Add soy sauce and mix. Immediately add the chicken broth. Cover with a lid and simmer for 3 minutes. Thicken the mixture with the cornstarch solution. Add the deep fried chicken pieces, mix and serve.

For variations substitute the chicken by pork, duck or goose. For tomato chicken balls, use the recipe for making tomato sauce as in tomato beef and then add the deep fried chicken pieces to the tomato sauce thus made.

CHICKEN EGG FOO YOUNG

½ cup sliced raw chicken breast
4 eggs
1 cup bean sprouts
¼ cup celery
¼ cup green onions
1 tbsp. soy sauce

⅛ tsp. Ac'cent
1 cup chicken broth
1 tsp. cornstarch dissolved in ½ cup water
Salt, pepper

Slice the celery diagonally into fine pieces and chop the green onions finely.

Heat 2 tbsp. peanut oil in a skillet until it smokes. Add a little salt. Add the chicken and mix for 1 minute. Add the celery, green onions and bean sprouts and mix for 30 seconds. Add the pepper, soy sauce and Ac'cent, mix and remove from the skillet. Add this mixture to a bowl containing 4 beaten eggs. Mix the eggs and vegetables well. Using 3-4 heaping tablespoons for each pattie, fry the patties on low heat. Each patty should be cooked less than a minute on each side. When patties are done, remove to a serving plate and arrange them in a row. Now add the chicken broth to the skillet. When the broth begins to boil, stir in enough of the cornstarch solution to thicken the broth. Pour this "gravy" over the egg patties before serving. For variations: Substitute the chicken with pork, beef, shrimp, lobster meat, crab meat or mushrooms. When bean sprouts are not available finely cut cabbage can be used. Lettuce can also be used but must not be saute before being added to the beaten eggs.

SHRIMPS IN LOBSTER SAUCE

Fresh shrimp, boiled and
   deveined
¼ cup salad oil
1 clove garlic, finely minced
½-¾ lb. pork, finely minced
⅛ tsp. Ac'cent
2 tsp. cornstarch

¼ cup soy sauce
1 tsp. sugar
Pepper to taste
2¼ cups boiling water
2 eggs
½ cup scallions and tops

Heat oil in a skillet with the cover. Add the garlic and pork and stir constantly until the pork is no longer pink. Prepare the cornstarch with ½ cup cold water. Stir soy sauce into pork mixture. Add the sugar, Ac'cent and boiling water and cornstarch. Bring gently to a boil. Reduce the heat to simmer. Stir until thick and translucent (about 10 minutes). Add the shrimps and cook for 5 minutes. Beat eggs slightly with a fork and add at once to gently bubbling mixture. Stir hard and fast .Remove in 2-5 minutes, add scallions and serve.

This recipe was contributed by Mrs. J. W. Slessor, who believes this has the qualities of a Chinese dish.

MUSHROOM SHRIMP BALLS

1 lb. fresh frozen shrimp
½ cup celery
½ cup bamboo shoots
5 waterchestnuts
5 Chinese mushrooms
1 tsp. garlic cloves, chopped
1 tsp. fresh ginger, chopped
½ cup water

1 tbsp. baking powder
⅓ cup flour
⅔ cup cornstarch
1 tbsp. soy sauce
1 tbsp. peanut oil
1 cup chicken broth
2 tbsp. cornstarch dissolved in ⅛
   cup water
Salt, pepper

Remove the shells from the shrimp. Make an incision down the back of the shrimp and remove the intestine, veins, etc. Wash. Mix the shrimp with a little salt, pepper, soy sauce and peanut oil. Make the batter with the cornstarch, flour, baking powder and ½ cup of water. Dip the individual shrimp into the batter and then deep fry at 375-400° F for 2 minutes. Place the shrimp on a paper towel to drain the excess oil. These shrimp can be served as such with a slice of lemon and are thus known as "Deep Fried Shrimp".

Peel and wash the waterchestnuts. Soak the Chinese mushrooms for at least 20 minutes. Cut all the vegetables into small pieces. Heat 2 tbsp. peanut oil in a skillet until it smokes. Add a little salt. Add the garlic and ginger and stir for 5 seconds. Add the celery and stir for another 10 seconds. Add the bamboo shoots, waterchestnuts and mushrooms and mix well. Add the chicken broth and simmer for 3 minutes. Thicken the mixture with the cornstarch solution. Add the shrimp balls minutes before serving.

Steamed Dishes

Dishes that are steamed are the easiest to prepare as long as you have a utensil like one used to cook a Christmas pudding. The process is generally used to cook meat dishes such as steamed garlic spareribs, mushroom steamed chicken or steamed shrimp sauce fish.

The steamed dishes usually consist of two types: 1. The "meat cake" dishes which use very finely chopped (almost like hamburger) pork, beef or fish together with the spices or flavoring agent used to designate the name of the particular dish.

An example of this type of dish is pork chopped with preserved duck's liver. The latter is a strong flavoring agent. With the pork, this flavoring agent would produce a dish known as "duck liver pork cake" or the English equivalent of duck's liver "porkburger". Instead of being fried and put between a bun like a hamburger, the Chinese would add a little salt, pepper, soy sauce and some complementary vegetables. This mixture is then spread on a plate and steamed for 10-15 minutes and served. One must make sure that there is a good supply of steam before the lid is placed on the pot. Otherwise the condensation would "flood" the meat dish. By substituting the duck's liver by salted pre-served fish, salted eggs, preserved chilied turnips, etc., a large variety of dishes can be produced.

2. This type of steamed dish uses meat such as chicken and spareribs which are cut into bite-size pieces, beef, which is usually thinly sliced, and fish (including shell fish), which is cut into chunks. Fish, when it is cooked, can easily be picked up in small pieces either by a fork or chopsticks. For this type of steamed dish, the meat is marinated with soy sauce plus a flavoring agent (thinly sliced) for 10-15 minutes before steaming. This type of dish is steamed for 15-20 minutes. The meat in this type is larger, so it must be cooked a bit longer. The steaming period is just as important as the time used to fry vegetables. Overcooking beef, fish or chicken is fatal but for pork it is immaterial. I cannot stress the exact time required to cook these meats. This will only "come with experience". People in North America generally eat their meat overcooked in comparison to the Chinese

dishes. Perhaps this is one of the reasons why North Americans attempts at "Chinese cooking" turns out slightly different than the dishes tasted in Chinese restaurants. (now you can become an "expert" by not overcooking).

An example of type two is mushroom steamed chicken. For this dish $\frac{1}{2}$-$\frac{3}{4}$ lb. of chicken breasts or legs, cut into bite-size pieces and 3-5 Chinese dried mushrooms, which have been soaked in cold water for 15-20 minutes, washed well and sliced into $\frac{1}{8}$-$\frac{1}{4}$ inch pieces, are used. If available, 3-5 fresh waterchestnuts, peeled, washed and sliced into $\frac{1}{8}$-$\frac{1}{4}$ inch pieces are also used. All the ingredients are placed in a bowl;then a tablespoon of chopped onion, and a tablespoon of chopped celery, if desired, one tablespoon of soy sauce, $\frac{1}{4}$ teaspoon of cornstarch and a little salt and pepper are added. All the ingredients are mixed well and are allowed to stand for at least 15 minutes before steaming.

Rarely do you need to steam chicken, fish or beef for more than 15 minutes.

GOLDEN NEEDLES AND RED DATES CHICKEN

$\frac{1}{2}$ of a 2-3 lb. fryer	2 stalks of green onions
5 waterchestnuts	1 tsp. cornstarch
5 Chinese mushrooms	1 tbsp. soy sauce
$\frac{1}{4}$ cup cloud ears	1 tsp. peanut oil
$\frac{1}{4}$ cup golden needles	Salt, pepper
5 red dates	

Cut the chicken into bite-size pieces. Soak the mushrooms at least 20 minutes before using. Soak the cloud ears and golden needles for a similar length of time. Slice the mushrooms thinly and cut the cloud ears into halves. Slice the red dates and remove the stones. Cut the stalks of green onions into $\frac{1}{2}$" lengths. Place the chicken in a bowl and mix with soy sauce, salt, pepper, peanut oil and cornstarch for 5-10 minutes. Add the other vegetables to the bowl and blend together. Place all the ingredients on a dish and spread to cover as much area as possible. Heat a steamer on high heat until there is an abundance of steam. Place the dish in the steamer for not more than 15 minutes. Serve.

STEAMED MUSHROOM CHICKEN

1 lb. breast of chicken or leg of chicken	1 tbsp. soy sauce
	1 tsp. peanut oil
5 waterchestnuts	$\frac{1}{2}$ tsp. cornstarch
5 Chinese mushrooms	Salt, pepper

Remove the bones from the chicken breast or legs and cut the meat into small pieces. Soak the mushrooms at least 20 minutes and slice thinly. Peel and wash the waterchestnuts and slice them. Mix all the ingredients in a bowl. Spread the mixture on a plate to cover as much area as possible. Heat a steamer on high heat until there is an abundance of steam. Place the plate in the steamer for not more than 4 minutes. Sprinkle green onions (chopped) on top before serving, if desired.

For variations duck meat can be substitute for the chicken. The waterchestnuts and mushrooms can be replaced by (a) universal sauce, (b) saang see jeung or other bean products, (c) shrimp sauce, (d) preserved turnips, plain or chilied, (e) sweet cucumbers.

STUFFED BITTER MELON

$\frac{1}{2}$ lb. pork

2 bitter melons

$\frac{1}{2}$ tsp. fresh ginger

1 tsp. garlic clove

$\frac{1}{4}$ cup onions

2 tsp. peanut oil

2 tbsp soy sauce

1 tbsp. black beans (dow see)

1 tsp. cornstarch

$\frac{1}{8}$ tsp. Ac'cent

Salt, pepper

Chop the pork, garlic, ginger and onions together to a consistency like hamburger. Mix in a bowl with the peanut oil, 1 tbsp. soy sauce, cornstarch, Ac'cent, salt and pepper. Cut the bitter melon into halves and remove the inner pulp and seeds. Rub the bitter melon inside and out with a sauce made from 1 tsp. soy sauce, 1 tbsp. black beans (pounded into a paste with the blunt end of a knife) and a little salt and pepper. Fill the melon cavity firmly with the meat mixture. Heat a steamer on high heat until there is an abundance of steam. Place the stuffed melon on a plate with the meat filled side up and place the plate in the steamer for 15 minutes. Serve when hot. The bitter melon is tender when cooked.

For a variation substitute the bitter melon by a vegetable spaghetti.

STEAMED CHINESE SAUSAGE

Chinese sausage, salted fish, soy sauce preserved duck and soy sauce preserved pork can be bought in all Chinese grocery stores. They are comparable to bacon or ham which is bought in super markets. These meats are very flavorful and tasty and can be cooked by placing a piece, that has been washed, on top of rice and steamed for 5-10 minutes and then cut into thin slices before serving.

Cooked on top of rice: After the rice has come to a boil and most of the water has been absorbed, place the meat on top of the rice. After 15-20 minutes, the meat is removed and cut into small pieces. With salted fish, use only a 1" wide x 3" long piece for each meal. Place one tablespoon of oil (°) on the spot where the fish was steamed on the rice and mix the rice well. Otherwise the rice will taste like fish. Also place 1 tsp. of oil on the salted fish before serving. It is a wonderful experience to taste salted fish, if you like strong cheese at all.

(°) For best results, heat 2 tbsp. of oil in a saucepan until it smokes, then cool before use.

STUFFED BEAN CURDS

3-4 bean curds
5 Chinese dried oysters
5 waterchestnuts
2 Chinese sausage
$\frac{1}{2}$ lb. fresh pork

1 tbsp. soy sauce
2 tbsp. oyster sauce
1 tsp. cornstarch
4 stalks of green onions

Soak the oysters for 1-2 hours and remove the contents of the "stomach". Peel and wash the waterchestnuts. Mince the oysters, waterchestnuts, Chinese sausage and pork and place in a bowl. Add the soy sauce and cornstarch and mix well. Cut the bean curds into quarters. Remove about 1 tsp. of bean curd from the center of each bean curd, quarter and replace it by some meat filling. Dip the green onions into boiling water (the green onions will be flexible). Use an onion leaf to wrap around the bean curd so that the filling will not fall out. Place the prepared bean curd on a plate and place the part of the bean curds that have been removed around the meat filled bean curds. Pour the oyster sauce on the bean curds. Heat a steamer until there is an abundance of steam and place the dish of bean curds in the steamer for 10 minutes. Serve while hot.

BLACK BEAN SHRIMP

1 lb. fresh frozen shrimp
  or prawns
3 stalks green onions
1 tsp. fresh ginger, chopped
1 tsp. garlic clove, chopped

1 tbsp. black beans (dow see)
$\frac{1}{2}$ tsp. cornstarch
1 tbsp. peanut oil
Salt, pepper
2 tbsp. soy sauce

Remove the shells from the shrimp. Make an incision down the back of the shrimp and remove the intestine and veins, etc. After the shrimp are cleaned, cut them into halves if very large ones are used. Cut the green onions into $\frac{1}{2}''$ pieces. Place the garlic, ginger and black beans (washed) in a cup and pound into a paste. Add the soy sauce to the cup and mix well. Place all the ingredients in the recipe in a bowl and marinate them for 15 minutes. Transfer this mixture to a plate (that will fit into the steamer) in such a way that the mixture will cover as much of the plate as possible (therefore the maximum area will be exposed to the steam). Heat the steamer on high heat until there is an abundance of steam. Place the plate in the steamer for 10 minutes. Serve.

During the 10 minutes there must be a fast generation of steam, otherwise you may get a dish of shrimp soup due to the excessive amount of condensation. When the dish is done, under fast steaming there should be a very small amount of water or juice in the plate due to a small amount of condensation.

For variations fresh crab or lobster can be substituted for the shrimp. Other bean products can be used in place of the dow see.

SHRIMP SAUCE COD FISH

1 2 to 3 lb. cod fish	2 tbsp. shrimp sauce
1 tsp. fresh ginger	1 tbsp. peanut oil
1 tsp. garlic clove	1 tbsp. soy sauce

Remove the scales, intestines and head of the fish and cut it into 2'' lengths. Rub the soy sauce on the fish. Chop the garlic and ginger as finely as possible and mix in a cup with the shrimp sauce. Shrimp sauce is a very salty paste which is slightly fermented and has a strong cheesy flavor. Coat the fish with this mixture and place it on a plate. When the steamer has reached full steam, transfer the prepared dish to the steamer and steam for 15 minutes. Pour 1 tbsp. of peanut oil on the steamed fish. Serve.

While serving this dish, an additional dish of "soy sauce" should be available if the fish is not salty enough. This sauce is made from 2 tsp. soy sauce, 2 tsp. peanut oil (°) and 1 tsp. finely chopped ginger.

(°) For best results, always heat some oil until it smokes, then cool before use. This is a standard technique in preparing oil for all seafood.

CHILIED TURNIP SHRIMP

1 lb. fresh, frozen shrimp
1 tsp. fresh ginger
$\frac{1}{2}$ cup green peppers
$\frac{1}{4}$ cup chilied turnips

$\frac{1}{2}$ tsp. cornstarch
1 tsp. soy sauce
1 tbsp. peanut oil
3 drops of sesame seed oil

Remove the shells from the shrimp and remove the intestines and veins, etc. After the shrimp are cleaned, cut them into halves. Wash the chilied (preserved) turnip thoroughly to remove the excess salt and slice the turnips as thinly as possible. Chop the green peppers and ginger together until quite fine. Mix all the ingredients together in a bowl. Place the mixture on a plate that will fit into the a steamer and spread all the ingredients on the plate to cover as much of the plate as possible. Heat the steamer on high heat until there is an abundance of steam. After 10 minutes of marinating, place the dish in the steamer and steam for 10 minutes. Sprinkle some finely chopped green onions on top before serving, if desired.

STEAMED STUFFED SEA CUCUMBER

1 large dried sea cucumber
$\frac{1}{2}$ cup chicken meat
$\frac{1}{2}$ cup lean pork
$\frac{1}{2}$ cup fresh shrimp
6 Chinese mushrooms
6 waterchestnuts
5 drops sesame seed oil
1 tbsp. fresh ginger

1 tbsp. garlic clove
3 tbsp. soy sauce
$\frac{1}{8}$ tsp. Ac'cent
1 tsp. sugar
4 tbsp. peanut oil
2 tsp. cornstarch
Salt, pepper

The dried sea cucumber should have a slit in the stomach where the intestines have been removed. Soak the sea cucumber in cold water until soft. Wash the inside daily to prevent rotting. (Sometimes it takes several days to soften the sea cucumber). Soak the mushrooms for 20 minutes before use. Peel and wash the waterchestnuts. Mince all the vegetables, shrimp, chicken and pork together. Add the soy sauce, Ac'cent, sugar, peanut oil, sesame seed oil, cornstarch, salt and pepper. Blend the mixture well. Place this filling inside the sea cucumber, wrap a piece of cheesecloth around the sea cucumber and tie securely with string to prevent the cucumber from shrinking into an irregular shape and forcing the filling out. It is also recommended to tie the cucumber onto the plate, with the filling side up, to prevent it from dropping into the water. Place this prepared dish in a steamer and steam for 1 hour. Make sure there is a lid on the steamer. Actually after $\frac{1}{2}$ hour, the cucumber is edible and slightly chewy. Remove the string and cheesecloth. Slice the cucumber diagonally into $\frac{1}{4}''$ in width pieces. Place the cut cucumber on the original plate. Spread some of the juice from the plate on the cucumber and serve.

STEAMED STUFFED CHINESE BUNS

Filling:

1 cup fillet of chicken

5 Chinese mushrooms

$\frac{1}{4}$ cup onions

1 tsp. garlic clove

1 cup raw pork

1 Chinese sausage

$\frac{1}{2}$ cup Chinese preserved pork

$\frac{1}{4}$ tsp. Ac'cent

2 tbsp. soy sauce

3 drops sesame seed oil

Salt, pepper

Bread dough:

1 pkg. of dry yeast dissolved in $\frac{1}{2}$ cup of warm water plus a pinch of sugar. After 10 minutes add $1\frac{1}{2}$ cups of milk. Measure about 4 cups of all purpose flour into a bowl and add $\frac{1}{2}$ tsp. of salt. Mix with the yeast solution. Mix until you have a smooth dough. Place the dough in an oiled bowl to rise. Place a little oil on the top of the dough and cover with a towel. After two hours in a warm place, the dough should be twice its volume. Knead the dough again with your hands using a little oil. Repeat the process at least three times.

In the meantime, soak the mushrooms for 20 minutes. Chop all the ingredients as finely as possible. Heat 2 tbsp. of peanut oil in a skillet until it smokes. Add the garlic, chicken, pork, Chinese preserved pork, Chinese sausage, onions and mushrooms and stir for 1-2 minutes. Remove the skillet from the heat and add the sesame seed oil, Ac'cent, soy sauce, a little salt and pepper. Mix and put the ingredients from the skillet into a bowl. Cut the bread dough into dinner roll size pieces, squeeze the dough flat and place 2 tbsp. of filling in each piece of dough. Seal the filling within the piece of dough, by bringing the edges towards the center. Place the dough, sealed side down, on a $4'' \times 4''$ piece of wax paper. Let the buns stand for a $\frac{1}{2}$ hour in a warm place. In the meantime, heat a steamer. Place as many buns as possible (at least $1''$ apart) on a plate that will fit into the steamer. Steam the buns for 20-30 minutes. Repeat the process until all the buns have been steamed. Serve the buns either hot or cold.

For variations: Fillings can be made with:

1. 1 whole salted egg yolk per bun,
2. barbecued pork or chicken meat only,
3. a boiled lima bean paste with sugar for sweet buns according to the following procedure: boil 2 cups of lima (or other) beans strain off the water and crush the beans. Squeeze the resulting bean paste through a strainer or cheese cloth to remove the skins. Add $\frac{1}{2}$ cup of sugar to the paste and mix well. Use this mixture for fillings. In making the bread dough for sweet Chinese buns, omit the $\frac{1}{2}$ tsp. of salt from the dough and add $\frac{1}{2}$ cup of sugar in its place.

STEAMED STUFFED CHINESE MUSHROOMS

$\frac{1}{2}$ lb. fresh, frozen shrimp
5 red dates
$\frac{1}{4}$ lb. pork with some fat
10-15 large Chinese mushrooms
3 dried Chinese oysters
1 tbsp. bean paste, semi-solid

3 tsp. soy sauce
4 tsp. peanut oil
1 tsp. cornstarch
1 tsp. fresh ginger
Salt, pepper

Remove the shells from the shrimp. Make an incision down the back of the shrimp and remove the intestines, veins, etc. Wash. Soak the oysters for 1-2 hours and remove the contents of the stomach. Wash well. Soak the mushrooms for at least 20 minutes. Mince the shrimp, pork and oysters together. Place in a bowl and add 1 tsp. peanut oil, 1 tsp. soy sauce, a little salt and pepper, the saang see jeung and 1 tsp. cornstarch. Blend all the ingredients together well. Slice the red dates and place on a separate dish for decorative use only. Remove the stems from the mushrooms and replace with 1-2 tsp. of the meat filling. Shape the filling like a semisphere. Place a few slices of red dates on each mushroom so that the red part will show. Place the mushrooms on a plate. Heat a steamer until there is an abundance of steam. Put the plate in the steamer for 20 minutes.

Heat 1 tbsp. of peanut oil in a sauce pan until it smokes (so that any peanut residue will be roasted). When cool, add 2 tsp. of soy sauce, and 1 tsp. finely chopped ginger and mix well. Sprinkle this oil mixture on the stuffed mushrooms before serving.

STEAMED EGG CUSTARD

2 cups boiling water
3 eggs
2 stalks of green onions
1 tsp. peanut oil

$\frac{1}{8}$ tsp. Ac'cent or
1 tsp. soy sauce
Salt, pepper

Cool the boiling water until it is luke warm. Beat the eggs in a bowl. Mix the water into the eggs and add the Ac'cent, salt, pepper, peanut oil and chopped green onions. Pour the egg mixture into a deep dish. Heat a steamer until there is an abundance of steam. Place the deep plate in the steamer for 10 minutes. Sprinkle 1 tsp. of soy sauce on top before serving.

For variations: Finely chopped Chinese sausage, duck, salted eggs, fresh pork or shrimp can be added.

STEAMED MEAT CAKES OR BALLS

½ lb. minced pork	3 tbsp. salted preserved turnips
5 waterchestnuts	1 tbsp. soy sauce
2 Chinese mushrooms	2 tsp. peanut oil
⅛ tsp. Ac'cent	1 tsp. cornstarch
1 small piece of Chinese orange	2 stalks green onions
peel (tangerine skin)	⅛ tsp. pepper

Soak the mushrooms for at least 20 minutes. Peel and wash the waterchestnuts. Wash the turnips to remove excess salt. Mince all the ingredients and mix well with the soy sauce, oil and cornstarch. Spread the mixture on a serving dish to cover as much area as possible so that the mixture is about ½'' thick or shape the mixture into meat balls about the size of golf balls. Heat a steamer until there is an abundance of steam. Place the dish in the steamer for 10-25 minutes.

For variations: substitute the turnip by one of the following: Chilied turnip, duck, duck liver, preserved pork, Chinese sausage, dried oysters (soak for 1-2 hours before use), salted eggs, salted fish and other spiced bean products.

STEAMED SALTED EGGS WITH PORK

½ cup pork with some fat	1 tsp. peanut oil
3 salted eggs	⅛ tsp. Ac'cent
1 stalk of green onions	Pepper

Mince the pork and place in a bowl. Clean and wash the black ash-coated eggs. Crack the shells and add the pork to the eggs. Use the fingers to squeeze the hard egg yolk into small pieces. Add the peanut oil, Ac'cent, pepper and chopped up green onions. Mix the ingredients well. Place the mixture on a serving dish. Heat a steamer on high heat until there is an abundance of steam. Place the dish in the steamer for 10-15 minutes. Sprinkle with 1 tsp. of soy sauce before serving.

STEAMED SWEET CUCUMBER WITH BEEF

½ lb. beef tenderloin or New York cut steak	1 tsp. soy sauce
½ cup sweet cucumber	½ tsp. cornstarch
2 drops sesame seed oil	1 tsp. peanut oil
	Salt, pepper

Slice the beef and sweet cucumber paper thin and place in a bowl. Add the sesame seed oil, soy sauce, cornstarch, peanut oil, salt and pepper. Mix well. Transfer the mixture to a serving dish. Heat a steamer on high heat until there is an abundance of steam. Place the dish in the steamer for not more than 3 minutes. Serve.

STEAMED GARLIC SPARERIBS

½ lb. spareribs	½ tsp. cornstarch
2 tsp. garlic cloves	⅛ tsp. Ac'cent
1 tsp. soy sauce	Pinch of pepper
½ tsp. fresh ginger	

Cut the spareribs into 1" x ½" pieces and place in a bowl. Add the finely chopped garlic, finely chopped ginger, soy sauce, Ac'cent, cornstarch and pepper. Mix well and marinate for 10 minutes. Place mixture in a serving dish. Heat a steamer on high heat until there is an abundance of steam. Place the dish in the steamer for 15 minutes. Sprinkle some chopped green onions on top before serving, if desired.

STEAMED WHOLE WINTER MELONS

1 winter melon, 1 ft. tall and 6-10" in diameter	2 small pieces orange peel (tangerine skin)
8 Chinese mushrooms	1 tsp. peanut oil
½ cup pork with some fat	2 tsp. soy sauce
1 cup chicken breasts	1 tsp. sugar
½ cup bacon or ham, if desired	⅛ tsp. Ac'cent
1 tsp. fresh ginger	1 pint chicken broth
1 tsp. garlic clove	Salt, pepper

Clean the outside of the winter melon with a brush. Cut 3" of melon off the top (use it as a lid) and remove the seeds and pulp. Tie the melon with a heavy string (like a basket) so that it can be dipped in and out of the pot. Soak the Chinese mushrooms for at least 20 minutes. Mince the chicken, pork, bacon or ham. Finely slice the mushrooms and chop the ginger, garlic and orange peel. Place all the ingredients in a bowl and add the sugar, soy sauce, peanut oil, Ac'cent, salt and pepper. Blend well. Place this mixture in the winter melon.

Add the chicken broth. The melon should be ¾ full. Otherwise add more chicken broth. Cover the melon with the "lid" portion. Place the melon in a pot. Place this pot in a larger pot and add water to the outer container until it is half full. Cover with a lid and steam for 2-3 hours or until the melon is transparent. Serve the solid contents hot and use the liquid as a soup. If soup is not desired, do not use any broth in steaming. Also note that the larger pot, used as a steamer is not needed if the melon is mature and no signs of cracks or punctures are present.

HAR GOW (Cat's Paw)

This is a shell-shaped pastry and consists of a type of chop suey filling enclosed in a rice flour skin (dough). Har Gow flour can be bought in Chinatown.

Filling:

6 Chinese mushrooms	2 drops sesame seed oil
½ cup celery	¼ tsp. Ac'cent
¼ cup onions	2 tbsp. soy sauce
2 tbsp. green onions	2 tbsp. peanut oil
1 cup fresh shrimp	Salt, pepper
1 cup raw pork	

Soak the mushrooms for at least 20 minutes. Chop separately the mushrooms, onions, green onions, celery, shrimp and pork as finely as possible but not into a paste.

Heat 2 tbsp. of peanut oil in a skillet until it smokes. Add a little salt. Add the onions, celery, pork and shrimp and mix for 30 seconds. Add the mushrooms and mix for another 30 seconds. Turn the heat off. Add the soy sauce, Ac'cent, sesame seed oil, pepper and green onions. Mix well and remove contents from the skillet to a bowl.

Har Gow dough: To 3 cups of Har Gow flour or rice flour in a bowl, add boiling water gradually, while stirring, until the dough is thick and heavy like pie dough. Cover the bowl with a plate for 10 minute so that the heat will cook the dough. Knead until smooth. Divide the dough into pieces of golf ball size. Roll each piece of dough with a well-oiled glass or rolling pin until extremely thin, about ⅛-¼ inch thick. Make sure the pieces are round in shape. Make pleats in one half of each piece of dough to form a pouch. The pleats are made by superimposing one part of dough on another. Place one heaping tbsp. of filling into the pouch. Fold the top half of the dough down to meet the pleated half and pinch the edges firmly until filling is firmly sealed within. Place the individual Har Gow (they look like cat's paws due to the pleated dough) on a dish which will fit into a steamer. Steam for 15 minutes. Repeat the steaming process until all Har Gow are cooked. Serve hot or cold. If the dough has a tendency to fall apart while pleating or while rolling into thin pieces, it is due to the fact that the dough has not cooked long enough or that the boiling water was poured too slowly and the bowl was too cold. A cure for this is to steam such dough (that will not pleat or roll) for 5 minutes and then repeat the rolling or pleating.

Barbecuing

This process is quite familiar in the North American home, and there is no need to go into it in too much detail. Generally it means that meat is cooked by direct heat such as broiling. If broiling is not possible, roasting would approach the state of barbecuing. Chinese barbecued dishes consist of pork, spareribs, chicken, ducks or geese. The main flavoring agents are soy sauce, sugar and barbecue powder. "Barbecue powder" is known as "heung new fun" in Chinese and is composed of the five fragrances listed here:

1. Star anise (Illicium anisatum). This is sometimes known as "Octagonal" spice and can be as large as an inch in diameter.

2. Flower buds of the Clove tree (Jambosa caryophyllus).

3. Anise-pepper or flower pepper (Xanthoxlum piperitum). This is one of the popular spices used for sea food.

4. Cinnamon (Cinnamomum cassia).

5. Fennel (Foeniculum vulgare).

There are two ways of getting the full effect of the spices used in Chinese cooking:

1. Direct method: this is done by simply marinating the meat, which is cut into the desired size, with the mixture of barbecue powder, soy sauce, sugar, salt, pepper, and sometimes a little sherry or whisky. This marinating is done for at least 15 minutes before starting to barbecue the meat. If barbecuing is done by means of a broiler, the meat is browned on one side and then turned over until the other side is brown. For bite-size pieces or strips of spareribs, it should not take more than 30 minutes for the barbecuing process. For a 3-4 lb. duck or chicken, it should not take more than 2 hours.

2. Indirect method: this is only used for whole fowl, because they have an inner surface. It is done by using the same spice mixture

as for the direct method but placing $\frac{3}{4}$ of the mixture inside the fowl and sealing the opening by string or metal fasteners. The other $\frac{1}{4}$ of the mixture is used to coat the outside of the fowl. It is also best to let the fowl sit for at least 15 minutes before barbecuing. The advantage of this method is that when the fowl is cooking, the flavoring spices inside the bird have no place to escape but permeate into the whole bird. The use of sugar provides a slightly sweet flavor to the outside of the pieces when they are cut. Therefore when the first morsel reaches your mouth, the first noticeable reaction of your taste buds is an awakening by such a coating.

BARBECUED SPARERIBS

1 lb. pork spareribs	1 tbsp. sugar
1 tsp. barbecue powder (Heung new fun)	$\frac{1}{2}$ tsp. garlic clove
	$\frac{1}{8}$ tsp. pepper
2 tbsp. soy sauce	$\frac{1}{2}$ tsp. salt

Cut the spareribs into $1'' \times \frac{1}{2}''$ pieces. Chop the garlic as finely as possible. Mix the garlic with the barbecue powder, soy sauce, sugar, salt, and pepper. Marinate the spareribs for at least 5 minutes with this mixture. Place the spareribs on a sheet of aluminum foil which is then place in the top of a cookie pan. (This saves scrubbing the pan later!) Cook the spareribs in the broiler for 10 minutes or until brown. Turn the spareribs over and cook for another 10 minutes.

It is quite acceptable to cook the spareribs in a "slab" but put slight cut between the bones to expose more surface area. Cut into bite-size pieces before serving.

While cooking the spareribs, look at them occasionally.

BARBECUED PORK

1 lb. leg of pork	1 tbsp. sugar
1 tsp. barbecue powder (Heung new fun)	$\frac{1}{4}$ tsp. salt
	$\frac{1}{4}$ tsp. pepper
2 tbsp. soy sauce	

Cut the pork into $2'' \times 2'' \times 5''$ pieces along the grain of the meat. Mix together the barbecue powder, soy sauce, sugar, salt and pepper. Marinate the pork in this mixture for 30 minutes. Place the pork on a sheet of aluminum foil which in turn is placed on a cookie pan. Broil for 10-15 minutes on each side. Use a baster when the pork appears dry, by dripping the fat from the aluminum foil over the pork. Slice the pork into $\frac{1}{8}-\frac{1}{4}''$ pieces before serving.

GOLD COINS (Chicken, Pork)

½ lb. pork tenderloin
½ lb. chicken breasts
3 tbsp. soy sauce
1 tbsp. barbecue powder
   (heung new fun)

1 tbsp. sugar
1 tsp. garlic clove, finely chopped
2 tbsp. sherry or rye
½ head lettuce

Cut the chicken and pork tenderloin into pieces about the size of silver dollars and about a ½" thick. Marinate them with the soy sauce, barbecue powder, sugar, garlic and sherry for a ½ hour. Place the chicken and pork alternately on the rotisserie, axis through the middle of the meat "coin". Cook for 10-15 minutes or until golden brown. Place the "coins" on a plate containing the finely cut lettuce.

BARBECUED DUCK

1-3 to 4 lb. duck
2 tsp. barbecue powder
   (heung new fun)
5 tbsp. soy sauce

2 tsp. sugar
½ tsp. salt
½ tsp. pepper
1 tsp. garlic clove, chopped

Wash the duck inside and out. Dry the duck with paper towels. Make a sauce consisting of the soy sauce, sugar, chopped garlic, barbecue powder, salt and pepper. Rub the duck inside and out with this sauce. Any excess sauce is put inside the duck. Use scewers to fasten the opening of the duck. Place the duck on aluminum foil on a roasting pan. Using the broiler element, place the duck about 6" from the heat. After 15-30 minutes, or when the duck is golden brown, carefully turn the duck over and continue to cook for another 15-30 minutes or until golden brown on this side also. Turn the element off and after another 20 to 30 minutes remove the duck from the oven. Cut a small slit in the stomach and drain the excess juice into a bowl. Cut the duck into bite-size pieces and pour the juice over the duck before serving. Total cooking period is 1½ hour.

It is quite acceptable to see some reddish color in the bones when cutting. This is the Chinese way of cooking. Chicken can be done in this way also.

Other variations: Using the same duck one can make the two following dishes from a barbecued duck:

1. Use only the thighs, drumsticks and wings for the barbecued dish.

2. Use the breast for either lichee nuts duck, dragon's eyes duck or pineapple duck according to the following recipe:

1 tin pineapple cubes, lichee
   nuts or dragon's eyes
¼ cup onions, chopped
1 tsp. fresh ginger, chopped
1 tbsp. vinegar

2 tsp. sugar
1 tbsp. cornstarch dissolved in ⅛
   cup water
Salt, pepper
Barbecued duck's breast

Heat 2 tbsp. peanut oil in a skillet until it smokes. Add a little salt. Add the ginger, and onions and mix for 30 seconds. Add the pineapple cubes and the pineapple juice, the vinegar and sugar. Mix. Thicken the mixture with some of the cornstarch solution. Cut the duck into bite-size pieces and place on a serving dish. Pour the pineapple mixture on top. Serve.

Sweet and sour tomato sauce is also an excellent sauce in place of the pineapple, lichee nuts or dragon's eyes, which come in cans like pineapple.

Deep Frying

Deep frying is not commonly done in Chinese homes, because there are so many other interesting ways of preparing a meal. Therefore there is no need to go into the extra expense of using so much oil to prepare a dish of deep fried food. The technique of deep frying is to make sure that the oil reaches a temperature of at least 375-400° F before starting to deep fry. The same idea also applies in not overcooking anything, eg. for shrimp or prawns it should not take more than 5 minutes. The only danger in overcooking is when the oil is not hot enough. For a 3-4 lb. fish it may take up to 20 minutes. It is quite common to deep fry the ingredients and then add the spices just before serving.

An example of this technique is deep fried rockcod which is prepared by using the whole fish. The scales are removed by tying a string to the tail, holding the fish up by this string and pouring boiling water over the fish. Thus the skin of the fish is also cooked. The scales can be wiped off with a paper towel. Then an incision is made in the stomach of the fish and the intestines, etc. are removed. The fish is then washed. Do not cut the head off (the head is the most delicious part of the entire fish). Now the whole fish is dried with paper towel again. Sprinkle some salt on the fish and dust it with some flour. When the oil in the deep fryer reaches 375-400° F, lower the fish into the oil. After 15-20 minutes, the fish should be nicely done and have a golden brown color. While the fish is being deep fried, a proper sauce should be prepared for it, eg. tomato sauce or sweet and sour sauce. These can be found in the recipes on frying.

DRIED SPARERIBS

1 lb. spareribs
½ tsp. barbecue powder
    (heung new fun)
⅛ tsp. pepper
½ tsp. garlic clove, chopped

1 tsp. soy sauce
4 tbsp. cornstarch
½ tsp. salt
1 egg

Cut the spareribs into 1" x ½" pieces. Place the spareribs in a bowl and add the barbecue powder, salt, pepper, finely chopped garlic and soy sauce. Mix well and let the spareribs marinate for 15 minutes. Mix in the beaten egg and add the cornstarch. Stir well until the spareribs are coated with the batter. Drop individual pieces into a deep fryer set at 375° F. After 15 minutes or when the spareribs are golden brown, remove them to a piece of paper towelling to drain some of the excess oil. Serve.

Some sweet and sour spareribs are made in the above fashion. The finished spareribs are placed in a sauce made from 1 pint of water, 1 tbsp. of vinegar, 2 tbsp. of sugar and ⅛ tsp. of Ac'cent. The sauce is thickened with cornstarch solution (1 tsp. cornstarch dissolved in ⅛ cup of water). The amount of sugar and vinegar can be adjusted to one's own taste and depends on the amount of sweet or sour desired.

DEEP FRIED PRAWNS

½ lb. prawns (shrimp), fresh,
    frozen
1 tsp. soy sauce
2 slices of lemon
⅔ cup cornstarch

⅓ cup flour
1 tbsp. baking powder
Salt, pepper
1 tsp. vinegar
½ cup water

Remove the shells from the prawns. Make an incision along the back and remove the veins, etc. Mix the shrimp with a little salt and pepper and the soy sauce. Prepare a batter by combining the cornstarch, flour, vinegar and baking powder with enough water to make a consistency like pancake batter. Make sure that the deep fryer is at 375°F before adding the baking powder to the batter. This is very important. If the batter sits too long after the baking powder is added, too much gas (carbon dioxide) is lost and you will not get a crisply cooked shrimp.

Dip individual shrimps into the batter and then put each into the deep fryer. After 1-2 minutes the shrimp should be golden brown. Remove the shrimps and place them on paper towelling to remove excess oil. Serve with slices of lemon.

For variations: This dish can be served with sweet and sour sauce or sweet and sour tomato sauce. Pineapple, lichee nuts or dragons eyes can be added to these sauces.

CANTONESE CHICKEN

1 2 to 3 lb. fryer
1 tbsp. soy sauce
$\frac{1}{2}$ tsp. barbecue powder
  (heung new fun)

2 tbsp. cornstarch
Salt, pepper

Clean the chicken and cut it into halves lengthwise. Sprinkle it with a little salt, pepper, the soy sauce and the barbecue powder. Let sit for 15 minutes. Sprinkle the chicken with the cornstarch to absorb any excess moisture. Hold the chicken half by one end and slowly lower it into the deep fryer which is at 375°F. If the chicken is put in the deep fryer too fast, the foaming (bubbling) action may produce a fire hazard. The chicken should be golden brown (cooked) in 3-5 minutes. Place the cooked chicken on paper towelling to remove any excess oil. Cut the chicken into bite-size pieces. Serve.

DEEP FRIED FISH WITH SWEET AND SOUR TOMATO SAUCE

1 3 to 4 lb. cod, bass or snapper
3 tbsp. soy sauce
3 tsp. cornstarch
2 tomatoes, cut into small pieces
1 tsp. garlic clove, chopped
1 tsp. fresh ginger, chopped

$\frac{1}{2}$ cup onions, chopped
1 tbsp. vinegar
2 tbsp. sugar
Salt, pepper
2 tbsp. cornstarch dissolved in $\frac{1}{2}$ cup water

Remove the scales, head and intestines of the fish. Put 4 cuts on either side of the fish about $\frac{1}{2}$" deep (to facilitate faster cooking). Rub the inside and outside of the fish with salt, pepper, 1 tbsp. soy sauce and 1 tbsp. cornstarch to absorb any excess moisture. Make sure that the deep fryer is between 375° and 400°F and cook the fish for 3 to 4 minutes.

While the fish is deep frying, prepare the sweet and sour tomato sauce by heating a skillet with 2 tbsp. of peanut oil until it smokes. Add the finely chopped ginger, finely chopped garlic, and onions. Stir for 30 seconds. Add the tomatoes, 2 tbsp. of soy sauce, salt, pepper, vinegar and sugar. When the mixture boils, thicken with the cornstarch solution to a consistency of gravy.

Sweet and sour tomato sauce is slightly sweeter than tomato sauce. This sauce can be used in place of other sauces in other recipes if desired.

EGG ROLLS

Filling for Egg Rolls

½ lb. fresh, frozen shrimp
¼ cup pork
¼ cup chicken
5 Chinese mushrooms
2 cups bean sprouts
5 waterchestnuts
½ cup bamboo shoots

½ cup onions
1 tsp. fresh ginger
½ tsp. sugar
1 tbsp. soy sauce
⅛ tsp. Ac'cent
Salt, pepper

Remove the shells from the shrimp. Make an incision along the back and remove the veins, etc., then slice the shrimp, chicken and pork. Soak the mushrooms at least 20 minutes. Peel and wash the waterchestnuts. Slice the mushrooms, waterchestnuts, onions and bamboo shoots into match stick sizes.

Heat 2 tbsp. of peanut oil in a skillet until it smokes. Add a little salt. Add the onions, ginger, shrimp, chicken and pork and mix for 1 minute. Add the mushrooms, bamboo shoots, bean sprouts, waterchestnuts, soy sauce, sugar, Ac'cent, salt, and pepper. Mix well and cover with a lid for 1 minute. Remove the mixture from the skillet and use below.

Egg Roll Batter

1 tbsp. flour
4 eggs
¼ tsp. salt

2 tbsp. water
Pinch of sugar

Mix the flour, egg, sugar, salt and water until smooth. Heat a skillet with a small amount of oil (spread out oil with some paper towel) under low heat. Add 2 tbsp. of batter to the skillet and immediately spread it to cover an area, 5-6" in diameter. After 1 minute or when set. It should be like an extremely thin pancake. When done, remove the egg roll "skin" to a plate and continue the process with the rest of the batter. Place 2-3 tbsp. of filling in the center of each "skin", making sure the filling is away from the sides. Fold in the opposite ends and then roll the skin into a cylinder. Secure the loose end of the skin with some uncooked batter (°) to seal the end. The idea is to make sure that the filling will not leak. Prepared egg rolls can be deep fried or fried in a skillet with ½ cup of oil until golden brown. Cut into bite-size pieces if desired before serving. Fried in a skillet is easier for the unexperienced cook.

(°) If crispy egg rolls are desired, dip the egg rolls into a batter made from the following before deep frying:

2/3 cup cornstarch
1/3 cup all purpose flour
1 egg

1 tbsp. baking powder
1/2 tsp. vinegar
1 cup water

Mix the egg, cornstarch and flour with enough water until smooth like thick gravy. Add the baking powder and vinegar. Mix well.

DEEP FRIED CHICKEN LIVERS AND GIZZARDS

1/2 lb. chicken livers
1/2 lb. chicken gizzards
2 tbsp. soy sauce
1/2 tsp. fresh ginger

1 tbsp. cornstarch
1/2 tsp. sugar
1 tbsp. green onions
Salt, pepper

Cut the chicken giblets into bite-size pieces and place them in a bowl. Add the soy sauce, finely chopped ginger, sugar, salt and pepper. Let the giblets marinate for 15 minutes and drain the excess juice. Mix the giblets with 1 tbsp. of cornstarch to absorb the excess moisture. Place individual pieces in a deep fryer, which is set at 375-400°F, for 3-4 minutes. The giblets should be dark brown. Place the giblets on paper towelling to drain excess oil. Sprinkle some finely chopped green onions on top before serving.

This dish is ideal to serve at a party or as a snack with a glass of beer.

Sweet and sour sauce, oyster sauce or tomato sauce, can be used to pour over the giblets before serving.

ALMOND CHICKEN

2 pairs breast of chickens
3/4 cup blanched almonds
2 tbsp. soy sauce

1 tbsp. cornstarch
1/8 tsp. Ac'cent
Salt, pepper

Bone the chicken and separate the four individual breasts from each other. Rub each breast with the 2 tbsp. of soy sauce, Ac'cent, salt and pepper. While the chicken is marinating (for 10 minutes), chop the almonds as finely as possible. Coat each chicken breast with almonds, by placing a handful of almonds on the chicken and pressing down with the palm of your hand. Do this on both sides of each chicken breast. Sprinkle some cornstarch on each chicken breast to absorb any excess moisture. Sometimes a beaten egg can be brushed on the chicken to make the almonds stick on easier. Place each breast in a deep fryer, set at 375-400°F, for 1-2 minutes. Do not cook for more than 3 minutes. Place the cooked breasts on paper towelling to drain off any excess oil. Cut into bite-size pieces. Serve while hot.

One may use some finely cut lettuce on the serving plate to aid in draining any excess oil.

Other technique: to the above almond coated chicken, add a batter coating made according to the batter for deep fried prawns, before deep frying.

WON TON SKINS (Wrappings)

2 cups all purpose flour
¼ tsp. salt

3 large eggs
⅓ cup water

Mix the flour and salt in a bowl. Mix ⅓ cup of water with 3 beaten eggs. Add this to the flour and mix by hand until the dough has the consistency of pie dough. Transfer the dough to a flour dusted pastry board and knead at least 30 times (the more the dough is kneaded, the better the Won Ton skins will be). Roll the dough out until it is ¼" thick. Cut the dough into 1" strips. Roll the 1" strips until paper thin (the thinner it is, the better the Won Ton skins will be). Cut the paper thin dough into squares approximately 3" x 3". This should make from 75-90 skins. These can be frozen up to three months if wrapped in wax paper and then a piece of wet cheesecloth.

DEEP FRIED WON TON

½ lb. pork
½ lb. fresh, frozen shrimp
10 waterchestnuts
¼ cup onions
2 tbsp. green onions

2 tbsp. soy sauce
Salt, pepper
Won Ton skins (ready made)
1 egg, beaten

Remove the shells from the shrimp. Make an incision along the back and remove the veins, etc. Peel and wash the waterchestnuts. Chop the pork, shrimp and vegetables as finely as possible and mix together. The mixture should look like hamburger. Put in a bowl and add the soy sauce, salt and pepper. Place a Won Ton skin in front of you so that one corner is pointing in your direction. Place about ½ tsp. of the mixture about ¼" from this corner. Fold this corner over twice with the meat inside. Take the two side edges and fold towards the rolled corners until they meet. Seal the edges firmly with a bit of beaten egg. Drop the individual Won Tons into a deep fryer set at 375-400°F for 2-3 minutes or until golden brown. Remove to a paper towel to remove any excess oil. Serve hot, or serve with sweet and sour sauce.

WON TON SOUP

Drop the individual Won Tons into a pot of boiling water rather than into a deep fryer. After 3-4 minutes remove the Won Tons with a slotted spoon into a pot of prepared, hot chicken broth. This should be made while the Won Ton is being prepared. Sprinkle with chopped green onions before serving.

DEEP FRIED GLUTEN WITH SWEET AND SOUR TOMATO SAUCE

Prepare the gluten according to the recipe for beef gluten and sweet and sour tomato sauce according to the recipe previously given.

Cut the gluten into $\frac{1}{2}$" x $\frac{1}{2}$" x 1" pieces and coat each piece with a little flour to absorb excess moisture. Place the individual pieces in a deep fryer that has previously been heated to 375°F. When the pieces have expanded and are golden brown, remove them from the deep fryer and place on a paper towel to drain off any excess oil. Then place the pieces on a serving plate and spread the sweet and sour tomato sauce over the pieces. Sprinkle some chopped green onions on top and serve immediately.

The deep fried gluten expand like pieces of sponge and can therefore absorb all the flavoring agents used in conjunction with them. Gluten is actually concentrated protein from the flour used to make them. Ac'cent or monosodium glutamate can be made from this gluten.

Variations: substitute the sweet and sour tomato sauce by oyster sauce, pineapple sweet and sour sauce, lichee nuts sweet and sour sauce. Gluten can be fried in a skillet for these dishes rather than being deep fried. The longer the gluten is fried, the more it will expand.

Soups & Combination Cooking
Frying--Deep Frying--Steaming

The above methods are created by me to explain the art of Chinese cooking. Do not be offended by the terminology I used. The only right words to describe the exact process would be the one written by a Chinese character. Prolonged cooking is usually done for soup when all the ingredients are either fried first or used as they are and then put into a pot with a sufficient amount of water. The soup is first brought to a boil and then simmered for $\frac{1}{2}$ hour to several hours. The soup thus prepared usually constitutes a distinctive dish. An example of this type of dish is bean curd soup with white nuts, red dates, mushrooms and golden needles plus a soup bone or chicken bone which are simmered in water for an hour. All Chinese soups are delicious and nutritious and must be treated as an integral part of a meal. There are quite a number of soups which can be prepared in less than a half hour. On the other hand there are some soups which require several hours to several days to prepare.

Another method of enhancing the flavor of Chinese soup is by heating a tbsp. of peanut oil until it smokes. Then a little chopped garlic and ginger is added to the oil, mix for 30 seconds. Then add the broth and other ingredients for the soup.

COUNTRY STYLE DUCK

1 3 to 4 lb. domestic duck	1 tsp. sugar
6 Chinese mushrooms	2 tbsp. soy sauce
1 cup onions, chopped	$\frac{1}{2}$ head lettuce
$\frac{1}{4}$ cup celery, chopped	3 tbsp. cornstarch dissolved in $\frac{1}{2}$ cup water
2 tsp. garlic clove, chopped	
1 tsp. barbecue powder (heung new fun)	Salt, pepper

Soak the mushrooms for at least 20 minutes before use. Clean the inside and outside of the duck. Rub the inside and outside of the duck with a sauce made from 2 tbsp. soy sauce, 1 tsp. barbecue powder, 1 tsp. sugar, a little salt and pepper.

Heat 2 tbsp. of peanut oil in a skillet until it smokes. Add a little salt. Add the garlic, onions, celery and mushrooms. Saute for 1 minute. Remove these vegetables from the skillet. Place the vegetables inside the duck and sew all the openings of the duck so that the juice will not leak out. Place the duck in a roaster and broil for 15 minutes or until the outside of the duck is golden brown. Transfer the roaster to the top of the stove and add enough water to cover about ¾ of the duck. Bring the water to a boil and cover with a lid. Simmer for 3 hours. Cut the lettuce finely and place on a large platter. Place the whole duck on the platter. Skim some of the fat from the roaster. Thicken the remaining juice with the cornstarch solution. Pour over the duck before serving.

EGG-FLOWER SWIRL SOUP

1 quart soup stock

1 tbsp. soy sauce

1 tsp. green onions, chopped

2 beaten eggs

¼ tsp. Ac'cent

1 tsp. peanut oil

A pinch of pepper

Bring the soup stock to a boil (this is made from any kind of soup bones). Add the soy sauce, Ac'cent, pepper and peanut oil. Turn the heat off. Stir in the green onions and eggs.

For variations: add ½ cup of fresh frozen peas to the soup stock and bring it to a boil for 3 minutes before adding the other ingredients.

CANTONESE EGG SWIRL SOUP

1 quart soup stock

5 Chinese mushrooms

¼ cup celery, sliced

¼ cup onions, sliced

½ cup minced pork

½ tsp. Ac'cent

1 beaten egg

1 tbsp. peanut oil

Salt, pepper

Make a soup stock from any kind of soup bone. Bring the soup stock to a boil. In the meantime heat 1 tbsp. peanut oil in a skillet until it smokes. Add a little salt. Add the pork and saute for 1 minute. Add the celery, onions and mushrooms. The mushrooms must be soaked for 20 minutes before use. (They must also be sliced thinly). Stir for another minute and transfer the vegetables to the soup stock. Simmer for 2 minutes. Add the Ac'cent and pepper. Turn the heat off and stir in the egg just before serving.

MUSTARD GREEN SOUP

1 lb. mustard greens
  (Chinese cabbage)
1 quart soup stock
$\frac{1}{4}$ tsp. Ac'cent

1 tsp. fresh ginger, chopped
1 tsp. peanut oil
1 tsp. soy sauce
Salt, pepper

Soup stock can be made from any kind of soup bones. Bring the stock to a boil and add the ginger, soy sauce, peanut oil, Ac'cent, salt and pepper. Slice the mustard greens (Diagonally about $\frac{1}{4}$-$\frac{1}{2}$" in width). Add the greens to the soup stock, cover and simmer for 5-10 minutes. Serve hot.

For variations: substitute mustard greens by buk choy, hop choy (sometimes also referred to as Chinese greens) or water cress.

SATIN FISH

1-3 to 5 lb. large boned fish
  (cod, bass, snapper, pike)
2 tsp. garlic clove, chopped
2 tsp. fresh ginger, chopped
$\frac{1}{2}$ tsp. orange peel
  (tangerine skin)
3 tbsp. peanut oil, heated until
  it smokes, then cooled

3 tbsp. soy sauce
2 quarts water
2 tomatoes
$\frac{1}{2}$ tsp. salt
$\frac{1}{4}$ tsp. pepper

Clean the fish—remove the head, scales and intestines. Boil 2 quarts of water in a pot and add the $\frac{1}{2}$ tsp. of salt, $\frac{1}{4}$ tsp. pepper and the $\frac{1}{2}$ tsp. of orange peel. Make sure the water is boiling, then add the fish to the water. Cover the pot with a lid (the water should cover the fish completely). Turn the heat off completely. After 20 minutes, a 5 lb. fish is done just right. While the fish is in the pot, prepare a sauce made from 3 tbsp. of soy sauce, the garlic, ginger and 1 tbsp. of heated peanut oil. Place the fish on a platter and slice the tomatoes, placing them in a ring around the fish. Spread 2 tbsp. of heated peanut oil on the fish, then spread the soy sauce mixture over the fish.

For variations use sweet and sour tomato sauce, oyster sauce or pineapple sweet and sour sauce instead of the soy sauce mixture. Other types of fish can be used if one does not mind picking the fine bones. A fish smaller than 3 lbs. requires only 10 minutes to "cook".

SATIN SPICE CHICKEN

2 prs. of chicken breasts
1 tsp. star anise
1 tsp. fresh ginger, chopped
1 tsp. anise seeds
1 tsp. soy sauce

2 cups water
1 tbsp. cornstarch dissolved in $\frac{1}{4}$ cup water
Salt, pepper

Cut each pair of chicken breasts into two pieces with the bone along the center. Rub the chicken with soy sauce. In a pot or deep fryer, boil 2 cups of water with the star anise, ginger, and anise seeds which are enclosed in a cheesecloth bag. Add a little salt and pepper. Simmer at least 20 minutes to extract the flavor from the spices. Remove the bag of spices. Bring the water to a boil and add the chicken. Cover with a lid. Turn the heat to low and leave for 5 minutes. Remove the chicken. Turn the heat to high to evaporate some of the water, if there seems to be an excess. Cut the chicken into bite-size pieces. Thicken the water with the cornstarch solution. Pour this "gravy" over the chicken before serving. Sprinkle some finely chopped green onion on the chicken, if desired.

SATIN ROAST CHICKEN

1 3 to 4 lb. fryer
$\frac{1}{2}$ cup onions
1 tsp. garlic clove, chopped
1 tsp. fresh ginger, chopped
6 Chinese mushrooms
$\frac{1}{2}$ cup bamboo shoots

5 waterchestnuts
1 tbsp. soy sauce
2 tbsp. cornstarch dissolved in $\frac{1}{8}$ cup water
1 cup water
Salt, pepper

Clean and dry the chicken. Soak the mushrooms for 20 minutes. Peel and wash the waterchestnuts. Slice the mushrooms, waterchestnuts, onions and bamboo shoots. Heat 2 tbsp. of peanut oil in a Dutch oven until it smokes. Add a little salt. Brown the chicken completely, not taking more than 15 minutes. Add the garlic, ginger, onions, mushrooms, bamboo shoots and waterchestnuts to the oven. Saute for 1 minute. Add the soy sauce, salt and pepper followed by 1 cup of water. Cover with a lid immediately. Simmer for 35-40 minutes. Remove the chicken and cut into bite-size pieces. Thicken the sauce in the oven with the cornstarch solution. Pour this sauce over the thicken before serving. Hot English mustard is ideal to use with this dish.

Note: If there is too much fat in the oven before the cornstarch solution is added, remove some of the fat before thickening.

ABALONE SOUP

½ cup canned abalone
5 Chinese mushrooms
1 tsp. fresh ginger, chopped
¼ cup celery, sliced
¼ cup onions, chopped
1 tbsp. soy sauce

1 cup raw pork, sliced
½ tsp. Ac'cent
1 quart water
2 tbsp. peanut oil
Salt, pepper

Soak the mushrooms for 20 minutes. Slice the mushrooms. Heat 2 tbsp. peanut oil in a skillet until it smokes. Add a little salt. Add the ginger and pork and sauce for 1 minute. Add the celery, onions and mushrooms, and stir for another minute. Turn off the heat and add the Ac'cent, soy sauce and a pinch of pepper. Add this mixture to a pot and add a quart of water. Bring to a boil and simmer for at least 5 minutes. Slice the abalone paper thin and add to the soup stock 1 minute before serving.

The water content of the canned abalone can be added to the water for extra flavor. Remember that the longer you simmer the mushrooms, the milder and sweeter the soup will become. The longer you cook the abalone, the tougher it will get.

LETTUCE AND FISH SOUP

½ lb. fillet of fish
1 tbsp. soy sauce
2 tsp. fresh ginger, chopped
2 tbsp. peanut oil
1 quart water

¼ tsp. Ac'cent
½ head of lettuce
3 drops sesame seed oil
Salt, pepper

Slice the fish and mix well with the soy sauce, Ac'cent, 1 tbsp. of peanut oil and a pinch of pepper. Slice the lettuce.

Heat a tbsp. of peanut oil in a pot until it smokes. Add a little salt. Add the ginger and mix for 20 seconds. Pour in 1 quart of water and bring to a boil. Add the sesame seed oil. Turn off the heat and add the lettuce. Stir for 10 seconds. Add the marinated fish and stir for another 10 seconds. Serve immediately.

SUBGUM SOUP

1 quart chicken broth
½ cup celery
¼ cup onions
½ cup chicken breasts, sliced

5 waterchestnuts
5 Chinese mushrooms
1 egg

Soak the mushrooms for 20 minutes. Peel and wash the water chestnuts. Slice the mushrooms, onions, celery and waterchestnuts. Add the mushrooms to 1 quart of chicken broth and bring to a boil. Simmer for 10 minutes. Add the waterchestnuts, celery, and onions. Simmer for 2-3 minutes. Turn the heat off and stir in the chicken. Add 1 egg and stir just before serving.

CHICKEN GIBLET SOUP

1 quart chicken broth	1 tbsp. soy sauce
1 cup chicken livers	$\frac{1}{2}$ tsp. salt
$\frac{1}{2}$ cup chicken gizzards	$\frac{1}{4}$ tsp. pepper
1 tsp. fresh ginger, chopped	$\frac{1}{2}$ lb. hop choy (swiss chard)
$\frac{1}{4}$ cup celery, chopped	2 tbsp. peanut oil

Slice the liver, gizzards and hop choy. Heat 2 tbsp. of peanut oil in a deep pot until it smokes. Add the ginger and celery and saute for 30 seconds. Add the chicken giblets and stir for another 30 seconds. Add the hop choy and mix for 30 seconds. Add the soy sauce, salt, pepper and chicken broth. Simmer for 15 minutes.

FRESH LOTUS SOUP

1 lb. fresh lotus roots	2 tbsp. peanut oil
1 tsp. fresh ginger	2 quarts water
$\frac{1}{2}$ tsp. tangerine skin	$\frac{1}{2}$ tsp. salt
$\frac{1}{2}$ lb. stewing beef	$\frac{1}{4}$ tsp. pepper
5 red dates	

Cut the beef into cubes. Soak the tangerine skin and the red dates for 20 minutes. Wash the lotus roots well. Remove the seeds from the red dates. Slice the lotus roots diagonally into $\frac{1}{4}''$ thick pieces. Crush the ginger in one piece. Do not cut the ginger by slicing. Heat 2 tbsp. of peanut oil in a deep pot until it smokes. Add the beef and saute for 1 minute. Add the ginger and mix for another 30 seconds. Add the 2 quarts of water and then add the lotus roots, red dates, tangerine skins, salt and pepper. Bring the soup to a boil and simmer for at least 2 hours before serving.

WINTER MELON SOUP

½ lb. winter melon
½ lb. lean pork
½ tsp. fresh ginger, chopped
3 pints broth, pork

1 tsp. soy sauce
2 tbsp. peanut oil
Salt, pepper

Remove the thick skin from the winter melon (this can be bought in small pieces in Chinatown). Slice the melon into ¼" thick pieces. Slice the pork thinly and add the soy sauce, salt and pepper. Heat 2 tbsp. of peanut oil in a deep pot until it smokes. Add the pork and saute for 1 minute. Add the ginger and mix for 30 seconds. Add the broth and bring the soup to a boil. Add the winter melon and simmer for 15-20 minutes.

For variations: Substitute the winter melon by hairy melon. This looks like a cucumber with hairs and is also available in Chinatown in season. When using this, scrape off the skin like you would do with carrots. Slice the hairy melon diagonally. One may also use bitter melon in place of the winter melon. This is also available, in season, in Chinatown. For bitter melon, you do not skin it. Cut the melon in halves and remove the pulp. Slice the melon diagonally. Soup using bitter melon has a slightly bitter taste. The Chinese refer to it as a "cool feeling" particularly in the hot summer.

SEA CUCUMBER SOUP

1 dried sea cucumber
6 Chinese mushrooms
1 tsp. fresh ginger, chopped
3 pints broth, pork
½ tsp. tangerine skin

½ cup lean pork
1 tbsp. soy sauce
2 tbsp. peanut oil
Salt, pepper

Dried sea cucumber must be soaked until soft, before use. This sometimes takes several days. While the sea cucumber is soaking, it must be throughly washed at least once a day and the water changed. This is done to prevent spoilage. Pay particular attention to the area where the stomach has been removed. Cooked cucumber tastes somewhat like soft rubber. It is not too chewy or tough and is noted for its texture and rarity rather than as a delicacy. If fresh sea cucumber is used, one need only remove the stomach and intestines. Wash it well with water and some salt and baking soda.

Slice the pork thinly and slice the cucumber into pieces about ¼" in thickness. Add the soy sauce to the pork and cucumber and sprinkle the mixture with a little salt and pepper. Soak the mushrooms for 20 minutes and then slice them thinly. Also soak the tangerine skin for 20 minutes before use.

Heat 2 tbsp. of peanut oil in a deep pot until it smokes. Add the ginger, pork and cucumber. Mix for 30 seconds. Add the 3 pints of broth, mushrooms and tangerine skin. Bring the soup to a boil and simmer for 30 minutes at least before serving.

EEL MAW SOUP

$\frac{1}{4}$ lb. expanded eel maw
6 Chinese mushrooms
1 tsp. fresh ginger, chopped
3 pints broth, pork

$\frac{1}{2}$ tsp. tangerine skin
$\frac{1}{2}$ cup lean pork
1 tbsp. soy sauce
2 tbsp. peanut oil
Salt, pepper

Eel maw comes in two forms, either expanded or unexpanded. The unexpanded one looks like a piece of translucent leather about $\frac{1}{4}$" thick. By deep frying under low heat, it becomes a 1" thick snow-white, foam-like material. It is noted for its texture and ability to absorb flavor in which it is cooked.

Soak the expanded eel maw for 30 minutes or until it is soft, before use. Squeeze the water out and cut it into $\frac{1}{2}$" widths diagonally. Soak the mushrooms for 20 minutes and slice them. Slice the pork into thin pieces and add the soy sauce and a little salt and pepper. Heat 2 tbsp. of peanut oil in a deep pot until it smokes. Add the ginger and pork and saute for 30 seconds. Add the 3 pints of broth and then add the mushrooms, tangerine skin and eel maw. Bring the soup to a boil and simmer for 30 minutes. Serve hot.

FRESH BEAN (Cake) CURD SOUP

2 cakes fresh bean curd
5 Chinese mushrooms
1 tbsp. salted preserved turnips
1 tbsp. peanut oil
$\frac{1}{2}$ cup sliced lean pork
1 tsp. fresh ginger, chopped

1 tsp. tangerine skin (gaw pay)
3 pints broth, pork
1 tbsp. soy sauce
1 tsp. green onions, chopped
Salt, pepper

Soak the mushrooms and tangerine skin for 20 minutes. Wash the turnip and slice it into thin pieces. Slice the mushrooms and chop the tangerine skin into small pieces. Cut each fresh bean curd into 6 pieces. Add the soy sauce to the pork and sprinkle the pork with a little salt and pepper.

Heat 1 tbsp. of peanut oil in a deep pot until it smokes. Add the chopped ginger and pork and saute for 30 seconds. Add 3 pints of broth. Bring it to a boil and add the tangerine skin, turnip, mushrooms and bean curds and simmer for 20-30 minutes. Sprinkle the green onions on top before serving. This soup can be served after simmering for 10 minutes if no Chinese mushrooms are used. Remember that the longer you simmer the Chinese mushrooms, the milder and sweeter the soup will become.

MUSHROOM BEAN CURD SOUP

2 cups dried bean curds
5 Chinese mushrooms
6 white nuts, if obtainable
4 red dates
2 tbsp. peanut oil

$\frac{1}{4}$ cup sliced lean pork
1 tbsp. soy sauce
1 tsp. fresh ginger, chopped
3 pints broth, pork or chicken
Salt, pepper

Soak the bean curds for 20 minutes as well as the mushrooms and red dates. Slice the mushrooms and red dates and remove the stones from the dates. Crack the white nuts and remove the hard shell. Use the nuts whole or slightly crushed. Mix the sliced pork with the soy sauce and add a little salt and pepper.

Heat 2 tbsp. of peanut oil in a deep pot until it smokes. Add the ginger and pork and saute for 30 seconds. Add the broth and bring the soup to a boil. Add the mushrooms, red dates, white nuts and bean curds. Simmer the soup for 30 minutes and serve hot.

White nuts are only obtainable in Chinatown. These nuts impart an unusual flavor to soup but require a little "getting used to" before they can really be enjoyed. When cooked, the white nut tastes somewhat like cooked new potatoes, with a slightly bitter flavor.

BIRD'S NEST SOUP

$1\frac{1}{2}$ cups dried bird's nest
8 cups chicken broth
$\frac{1}{2}$ cup chicken breasts
2 egg whites, beaten

1 tsp. cornstarch dissolved in $\frac{1}{2}$ cup water
1 tsp. salt
$\frac{1}{4}$ cup cooked ham (optional)

Soak the dried bird's nest for at least 6 hours before use. Strain off all the water from the softened bird's nest. Rinse well several times and remove any feathers present. The chicken broth should be made from chicken necks and bones that have been boiled for 3 hours although chicken concentrate can be used if necessary. Make sure that the broth is free from bones by straining. Chop the chicken breasts as finely as possible and mix with the beaten egg whites. Place the bird's nest in the broth and cook for at least 30 minutes. Add, while stirring, the chicken breast-egg white mixture. Simmer for 1-2 minutes. Add the cornstarch solution to slightly thicken the soup (that is enough of the cornstarch solution to make the soup slightly thick). Garnish the soup with the finely chopped ham, if desired before serving.

For variations: substitute the bird's nest by shark's fin. This must also be soaked for at least 6 hours before use.

For best results, the bird's nest or shark's fin, should be simmered for 3 hours before serving.

BEEF CONGEE

1 cup rice

2 quarts water

2 tbsp. soy sauce

1 tbsp. peanut oil*

5 drops sesame seed oil

1/4 tsp. Ac'cent

1/2 lb. beef

1 tbsp. preserved salted turnip
(choong choy)

1 tsp. fresh ginger

1/2 tsp. tangerine skin (gaw pay)

1 tbsp. green onions

Salt, pepper

Congee is somewhat like porridge but is made from rice and a variety of flavoring agents. It can be served as a snack or as a light meal all by itself. I have found it to be excellent for Sunday dinner.

Soak the tangerine skin for 20 minutes. Wash the rice until it is relatively clear. Add 2 quarts of water and 1/2 tsp. of salt. Bring the water to a boil and add 1 tbsp. of peanut oil. While the water is coming to a boil, chop the tangerine skin and ginger finely. Put them in the boiling rice and simmer for 1 1/2 hours, stirring occasionally to prevent burning on the bottom of the pot. Slice the beef paper thin. Wash and chop the preserved turnip finely, mix with the beef, add the soy sauce, sesame seed oil, Ac'cent, chopped green onions, salt and pepper. Add this beef mixture seconds before serving.

Variations: Substitute beef by (1) sliced fillet of cod, bass or snapper (2) shrimp or pork. If either of these two are used, one would simmer for 5 minutes more after the addition to the simmering rice, before serving. *Heat oil until it smokes and then cool before use.

DUCK'S WING CONGEE

1 cup rice

2 quarts water

2 tbsp. soy sauce

2 tbsp. peanut oil

5 drops sesame seed oil

1/4 tsp. Ac'cent

1/2 lb. preserved duck's wings or feet

1 tbsp. preserved salted turnip

1 tsp. fresh ginger

1/2 tsp. tangerine skin (gaw pay)

1 tbsp. green onions

Salt, pepper

Soak the tangerine skin for 20 minutes. Wash the turnip and duck's wings or feet. Chop the ginger and turnip finely. Cut the duck's wings at the joints. Wash the rice until reasonably clear. Add 2 quarts of water. Bring it to a boil and add 1/2 tsp. salt, the duck's wings or feet, tangerine skin, turnip, ginger, Ac'cent, peanut oil, sesame seed oil, salt and pepper. Simmer the mixture for 1½ hours. Add the soy sauce, and chopped green onions seconds before serving.

The flavor from this preserved duck's feet is sometimes beyond description. It is a must in the introduction into Chinese cooking. If you enjoy Chinese cooking at all, you should like this. The longer you simmer your congee, the more flavorful it will become, but you may have to add more boiling water to thin it down before serving.

Variations: substitute duck's feet by ½ lb. shelled white nuts and ½ lb. beef tripe.

Rice & Noodles

STEAMED WHITE RICE

When measuring rice for a Chinese meal, use a minimum of ½ cup of raw rice per person. In a Chinese diet, 8 oz. of rice per person per meal is consumed, on the average. Always use long grain (unconverted) rice with a Chinese meal.

The rice is washed by rubbing it between two hands in a pot. The milky water is drained off and fresh water is added. The process is repeated about 5 times (at a minimum) or until the water is relatively clear. When this stage is reached, add enough water so that it is about ¾ of an inch above the level of the rice. The rice is then brought to a rapid boil and kept boiling for 4-5 minutes. If foaming occurs, open the lid slightly. The rice is then simmered for about 20 minutes under low heat with the lid tightly closed. Never open the lid during this time. This way of cooking will produce a crust on the bottom of the pot—it is a standard Chinese way of cooking rice. This crust can be eaten by adding ½ cup of water to the pot after most of the rice has been removed. The water is spread around the pot. This is allowed to soak for 15-20 minutes.

A non-Chinese practice can be followed. This is the addition of 1 tsp. of butter or oil to the rice before simmering under low heat and reducing the boiling under high heat from 4-5 minutes to 2-3 minutes. No crust will form on the bottom if this method is used.

If the rice is primarily used for fried rice, use slightly less water to cook the rice. This way the rice will be firmer. Some people often use day old rice for fried rice although this practice is not necessary.

CHICKEN FRIED RICE

$\frac{1}{2}$ cup raw chicken
5 cups cooked rice
$\frac{1}{2}$ cup onions, finely chopped
$\frac{1}{4}$ cup celery, finely chopped
1 tbsp. green onions, chopped

4 tsp. soy sauce
$\frac{1}{8}$ tsp. Ac'cent
2 tbsp. peanut oil
2 eggs
Salt, pepper

Slice the raw chicken thinly and mix with 1 tsp. soy sauce and a little salt and pepper. Heat 2 tbsp. of peanut oil in a skillet until it smokes. Add a little salt. Add the chicken and saute for 1 minute. Add the celery and onions and stir for another $\frac{1}{2}$ minute. Turn the heat to low and add the rice. Mix well until the rice is hot. Add the green onions, soy sauce, Ac'cent and 2 eggs. Mix well and serve.

For variations: substitute chicken by raw pork, barbecued pork, shrimp or vegetables such as broccoli, cabbage or green peppers.

BEEF FRIED RICE

$\frac{1}{2}$ cup raw beef (sirloin)
5 cups cooked rice
$\frac{1}{2}$ cup onions, finely chopped
$\frac{1}{4}$ cup celery, finely chopped
1 tsp. fresh ginger, chopped
4 tbsp. soy sauce
1 tbsp. green onions, chopped

2 tsp. cornstarch
1 cup water
3 tbsp. peanut oil
$\frac{1}{8}$ tsp. Ac'cent
2 eggs
Salt, pepper

Slice the beef paper thin and mix with 1 tsp. soy sauce, ginger, cornstarch, Ac'cent and a pinch of pepper. Heat 2 tbsp. of peanut oil in a skillet until it smokes. Add a little salt. Add the beef and saute for 5 seconds. Add 1 cup of water (watch for the immediate rise of steam). Remove the skillet from the heat source and take the beef out of the skillet. The beef should be coated with a gravy-like sauce. If all the water has evaporated, add a little more water until the "gravy" is seen (before removing the beef from the skillet). Rinse the skillet with water and heat until dry. Add 1 tbsp. of peanut oil and heat the skillet until it smokes. Add the celery and onions and mix for 30 seconds. Turn the heat to low and add the rice. Mix well until the rice is hot. Add the green onions, the rest of the soy sauce and the eggs. Mix well.

Remove the rice from the skillet and place it on a serving dish. Pour the cooked beef and sauce on top of the rice.

Variations: Substitute the cooked beef and sauce by sweet and sour tomato sauce (see the sweet and sour tomato sauce recipe). For mushroom fried rice, omit the beef and add 1 cup of Chinese mushrooms that have been soaked for 20 minutes before use. The mushrooms should be added after the addition of the onions and celery. Mix for 1 minute instead of a $\frac{1}{2}$ minute because the mushrooms can stand a little extra cooking.

BEEF CURRIED WHITE RICE

$\frac{1}{2}$ cup raw beef

5 cups cooked rice, hot

$\frac{1}{2}$ cup onions, chopped

$\frac{1}{4}$ cup celery, chopped

1 tsp. fresh ginger, chopped

1 tbsp. soy sauce

$\frac{1}{8}$ tsp. Ac'cent

2 tbsp. peanut oil

1 tbsp. curry powder

$\frac{1}{2}$ tsp. chili powder (optional)

2 cups water

2 tbsp. cornstarch dissolved in $\frac{1}{2}$ cup water

Slice the beef paper thin. Heat 2 tbp. of peanut oil in a skillet until it smokes. Add the ginger and beef and saute for 5 seconds. Remove the ginger and beef from the skillet. Add the onions and celery and mix for $\frac{1}{2}$ minute. Turn the heat to low and add the soy sauce, Ac'cent, curry powder, chili powder, salt and pepper followed by 2 cups of water. Bring the mixture to a boil and thicken it with the cornstarch solution. Add beef, and mix well. Pour this on top of the cooked rice.

CHICKEN NOODLE SOUP

1 lb. fresh noodles

$\frac{1}{2}$ cup raw chicken

3 pints chicken broth

1 tsp. soy sauce

2 tbsp. peanut oil

2 tbsp. chopped green onions

2 quarts water

Salt, pepper

Two processes are involved in making chicken noodle soup:

1. Cook the noodles in a separate pot with boiling water to remove the excess starch.

2. After a broth has been prepared, the cooked noodles are transferred into the broth pot. The soup should be clear and thin—a typical Chinese soup.

Me hods: Bring 2 quarts of water to a boil and add the noodles. Boil for three minutes and drain off the water.

While the noodles are boiling, cut the chicken into match-stick size pieces. Mix with the soy sauce, peanut oil and a little salt and pepper.

Heat a deep pot with 1 tbsp. of peanut oil until it smokes. Add a little salt. Add the chicken and mix for 30 seconds. Add the chicken broth and bring to a boil. Add the cooked noodles and stir for 30 seconds. Sprinkle the green onions on top before serving.

Dried noodles can be substituted for fresh noodles but the dried noodles must be boiled in water for at least 15 minutes or until tender before draining off the water.

For variations: Wor mein—this is made by adding the following additional ingredients to the chicken broth:

1 cup hop choy or swiss chard
$\frac{1}{2}$ cup chicken giblets (liver, gizzards)
$\frac{1}{2}$ cup squid (soaked in water until soft—at least 2 hours)
$\frac{1}{2}$ cup bamboo shoots
5 water chestnuts (washed and peeled and chopped)
5 Chinese mushrooms (soaked for 20 minutes before use).

CANTONESE (Chicken) CHOW MEIN

$\frac{1}{2}$ lb. fresh Chinese egg noodles
1 cup fresh fillet of chicken
$\frac{1}{2}$ cup onions
$\frac{1}{2}$ cup celery
2 cups bean sprouts
2 Chinese mushrooms
$\frac{1}{2}$ cup water
3 tsp. soy sauce

$\frac{1}{8}$ tsp. Ac'cer t
$\frac{1}{2}$ tsp. fresh ginger, chopped
$\frac{1}{2}$ tsp. garlic clove, chopped
$\frac{1}{2}$ cup peanut oil
1 tsp. cornstarch dissolved in $\frac{1}{8}$ cup water
Salt, pepper
A pinch of sugar

Soak the mushrooms for at least 20 minutes. Slice the mushrooms, onions and celery somewhat like match-sticks. Slice the chicken paper thin. Mix the chicken with 1 tsp. of soy sauce, add pinch of salt and pepper.

Heat 2 tbsp. of peanut oil in a skillet until it smokes. Add a little salt. Add a small portion of the noodles and fry for 10 seconds. Turn the noodles over and fry for another 10 seconds. Remove the noodles from the skillet. Add a little more oil and repeat the process until all the noodles are fried to a golden hue.

Heat the skillet until it smokes with 2 tbsp. of peanut oil. Add the garlic and ginger and then the chicken and saute for 30 seconds, add the celery, onions, mushrooms and bean sprouts. Stir after each addition. After 1 minute add 2 tsp. of soy sauce, Ac'cent, sugar, and $\frac{1}{2}$ cup of water. Immediately cover the skillet with a lid and steam for another minute. Thicken the water, if any, with the cornstarch solution. Add the noodles to the skillet. Turn the heat off. Mix well and cover the skillet with a lid until the noodles soften. Serve.

Tea

Tea is an important item in every Chinese home and is always drunk after a meal. The tea is served either hot or lukewarm. It is a general rule that when a family arises in the morning, the making of a pot of tea takes precedent over everything else. This pot of tea is placed in a straw packed container which acts as an insulator to keep the tea hot. During the course of the day, if one is thirsty, he knows where the tea pot is kept. Both adults and children are tea drinkers since water is never recommended to quench one's thirst. Tea is not only looked upon as a refreshment but is also drunk for its "medicinal" value. For example, Po Nay Chaah (tea) is known for its ability to dissolve or disperse fat in the body system. Thus it is believed that any excess fat will be in constant circulation in the blood stream so it is not possible for it to deposit in any particular spot. Perhaps the term "fat" also includes cholesterol. This is why Po Nay Chaah is popular particularly after a rich meal. Since I am a chemist, I do not take these beliefs seriously but I automatically have a cup of good strong Po Nay Chaah after a rich meal, without any questions as to its value or to the legend involved in the Chinese people's idea of the value of a cup of tea.

Chinese tea is distinct in variety, unlike Western tea, which is somewhat the same, except that it is packaged by a different company under different brand names.

The names of Chinese tea are derived from the area where the tea is best grown. The following are some examples of the most common teas used by the Chinese people:

1. Wun Moo Chaah (Cloud Mist green tea).
This tea is grown on the mountain peaks in the province of Kiangsi in China. Men have never seen how these tea shrubs are grown because they are at such a high altitude. Only trained monkeys are used to pick the leaves of this plant. The high price of this tea may be due to the scarcity of such a tea. Perhaps the monkeys are more interested in play than in work while on the mountain peaks!

2. Loong Jang and Heung Pien Chaah (Dragon's well and Fragrant Petals tea). These are both green tea from the province of Chinkiang.

3. Po Nay Chaah is a reddish-black tea from the province of Yunnan. This tea is supposed to be a tonic type of tea and comes in

the form of a round cake about 1" thick and 6" in diameter or in a loose form in a box.

4. Oolong, Suy Sien, Ngun Jum and Sao May Chaah (Black Dragon, Water Nymph, Silver Needles and Eyebrows of Longevity tea) are the common green teas from the province of Kwangtung.

Chinese tea should be stored in a closed container to prevent it from absorbing any other odors and to reduce the chances of losing its fragrance.

The normal way of making Chinese tea is to rinse the tea pot with boiling water and add the tea leaves to the pot (about 1 tbsp. per cup of tea) before adding the boiling water to make the tea. In the restaurants in China a tea pot is filled about a $\frac{1}{4}$ full of tea leaves. The waiter comes around continuously with boiling water to fill the tea pot as soon as you have had your first cup of tea. Four to five fillings with hot water to the same tea leaves is the normal practice. To really enjoy a cup of Chinese tea, one should never use cream or sugar.

Wong Law Kete Chaah

This is a medicinal "tea" invented by Mr. Law Kete Wong, a herbalist. A person always asks for this type of tea, which is composed of about six different herbs, for the relief of stomach upsets after a period of great indulgence in rich foods such as barbecued pork (with fat) or after a meal with a particularly high fat content. This tea is available in all Chinese drugstores.

My aunt loved rich foods and as a result had many stomach ailments. About five years ago, it was discovered by X-ray diagnosis, that she had numerous gall stones. An operation was scheduled in a month's time. How frightened she was at the thought of an operation! Thus she rushed to the nearest city and bought a good supply of the Wong Law Kete Chaah. For the next month, she drank this medicinal tea in place of ordinary tea. Two days before the operation was to be performed, she told the doctor that she no longer suffered any pain. Thus another set of X-rays was taken. This time no gall stones were found. All the doctor could say was "I just cannot understand it!"

Another tea, Po Nay Chaah, a regular household tea, is thought to have the same effect but in a milder form. This tea is favored by some fat people, particularly those who may be suffering from high blood pressure.

Miscellany

ALMOND PUDDING

1 cup slightly roasted almonds (blanched)
1 quart water
1 pint milk

½ cup sugar
¼ cup cornstarch dissolved in ½ cup water
1 tsp. vanilla

Use a Waring blender to reduce the almonds to a fine suspension in some of the water. Add this to a pot containing the rest of the water and the milk. Add the sugar and vanilla. Bring the mixture to a boil and thicken it with the cornstarch solution until it has the consistency of gravy. Serve hot or cold.

For variations: Substitute the almonds by slightly roasted sesame seeds. Also use a Waring blender to reduce the seeds to a fine suspension.

Although there is no such dish as a dessert in Chinese meals, there is a proverb that states one always eats his fruit after a meal. So this pudding can be served as either a dessert or as a snack.

100 YEAR OLD EGGS

6 parts of ashes
1 part agricultural lime
1 part salt peter or potassium nitrate
½ tsp. salt per egg
1 lb. tea leaves
Use large eggs such as duck, turkey, etc.

Brew a strong tea and use this tea to mix the above ingredients to the consistency of a mud-pie. Cover each egg with at least a ½ inch of the mixture. Place the eggs in a large container with 2 inches of earth on the bottom. Have the eggs 2 inches apart. Fill the spaces between the eggs with more earth. Place 2 inches of earth on top of the eggs. Set the container in a dark, cool place for 100 days. Before serving, wash off the coating and remove the egg shell. Cut the eggs into halves and serve with sweet and sour ginger by placing slices of ginger alternately with the eggs.

The eggs should have the appearance of 3 minute boiled eggs except the color is greyish-black to transparent black.

HOW TO SPROUT BEAN SPROUTS

Bean sprouts are made from mung beans which are green in color and about $\frac{1}{8}$" x $\frac{1}{8}$" x $\frac{1}{4}$" in size. The beans cost 25 cents a pound and one pound of beans will produce 5 pounds of bean sprouts. Good results can normally be obtained by keeping the beans moist during the sprouting period and rinsing off the stagnant water every day. In commercial practice, the beans are first scalded with boiling water. The beans are then watered every four hours, day and night, and are kept in a container with holes in the bottom to drain off the excess water.

Here is what can be done to produce reasonable bean sprouts:

1. Pour hot water into a pot containing 1 cup of beans. Leave the water on the beans for 30 seconds then drain the water off. Add cold water to cover the beans.

2. Place the beans in a warm (not hot) place.

3. At least every 24 hours fill the pot with water and drain all the water off. Repeat the process twice to remove all stagnant water. While the beans are sitting in the warm place, place a piece of cheesecloth over the top of the pot to retain moisture.

4. The bean sprouts will be ready in 5 days if kept in a warm place and in 7 days if kept in a cool place.

SOME TALES INVOLVING CHINESE COOKING

Winter Melon

It has been said that when one eats too much of "hot air effects" foods such as deep fried or barbecued dishes, one will eventually suffer some kind of stomach upset, sore throat or other type of minor discomfort. Evidence of such a discomfort can be strongly colored phlegm when coughing, impurities found in the corners of the eyes in the morning and strongly colored urine.

When this happens, the Chinese have found that winter melon soup has helped the situation. This soup consists of 2 pounds of winter melon, 1 pound of stewing beef, 1 teaspoon of tangerine skin, 1 teaspoon of ginger and 5 dried oysters which are simmered together for 3 to 6 hours. This soup is supposed to be a "cool air effect" soup and will thus neutralize the "hot air effect". I often have this soup when my son or I have a sore throat and it seems to work, believe it or not!

Water Cress Soup

Once upon a time an elderly man was sent into the swamp to die. He was suffering from tuberculosis and the doctor had given him one month to live. While he was out there he said to himself "If I am going to die there is no point in wasting rice by eating it." Therefore he gave all his rice to friends and relatives whom he felt could use it more meaningfully than he would himself. While waiting to die he came to a very green spot in the swamp. Here he decided to rest. While resting, the old man began to chew on a piece of a green plant that grew nearby. To his surprise, the plant had a rather pleasant taste. So he decided to remain in this spot and while here he ate these plants. Much to his surprise, after a few days of eating these plants, he discovered that he coughed less and less. In fact he seemed to be getting stronger. After the month had passed, he was amazingly healthy. So he decided to go home to check with his doctor as to why he was still alive. To the doctor's amazement, the old man was no longer suffering from tuberculosis.

To this day, the green plant, known as water cress is thought to be able to keep one's lungs moist. Thus water cress soup has been widely accepted as a very good soup.

Glossary

abalone.   A single-shelled mollusk that clings tenaciously to rocks in the ocean. Dried abalone is used mostly in soups, canned abalone as a meat dish. Prolonged cooking tends to toughen it.

Ac'cent.   One of the trade names for monosodium glutamate, q.v.

bacon, Chinese.   Very delicious pork that has been preserved with salt, sugar, and soy sauce, used as a meat dish or for adding flavor to other meat dishes.

bamboo shoots.   The tender young shoots of various kinds of bamboo. They are delicately flavored and maintain their crispness when cooked—a welcome addition to many stewed, steamed, or simmered dishes.

bean curd.   This is available fresh, dried, or fermented. It is prepared from soy beans, has a very high protein content, and is widely used in Asiatic countries.

been paste.   See: chili bean paste.

bean sauce.   See: red bean sauce.

bean threads.   These are made from powdered mung beans, and their thin, long transparent strands resemble nylon. They absorb a remarkable amount of liquid. Known by many names such as: cellophane noodles, fun see, harusame, long rice, oriental vermicelli, translucent noodles.

beans, black.   When partially fermented and salted they are known as dow see and are used for flavoring.

birds' nests.   Nests of a special kind of swallow having highly developed salivary glands. They predigest the spawn of fish and oceanic vegetation and use this to build their nests, hidden away in almost inaccessible caverns. The most expensive are those that have not yet been used, are pure white in color, and are relatively free from tiny feathers.

black beans.   See: beans, black.

cellophane noodles.   See: bean threads.

chestnuts.   See: water chestnuts.

chili bean paste.   A sweet, hot flavoring known as hoi sien sauce.

Chinese bacon. See: bacon, Chinese.
Chinese radish. See: radish, Chinese.
Chinese sausage. See: sausage, Chinese.
Chinese vinegar. See: vinegar, Chinese.
chung choy. See: turnips, preserved.
cloud ears. A fungus, like mushrooms, slightly crisp when cooked, used for flavoring. Known as wun zee.
congee. A thick soup. Also known as joke.

dates, red. Slightly sweet, dried oriental dates used in flavoring soups and meat dishes. Known as hong daw.
dong gaw. See: melon, winter.
dow see. Partially fermented, dried black beans used for flavoring.
dragon's eyes. See: longans.

eel maw. The extended stomach of an eel, used in soups.

fish, salted. Fish that has been preserved in salt. Used as a meat dish, or in flavoring other dishes, or steamed on top of rice. Must be washed thoroughly before using, and even so it is too salty to be eaten like salmon or kippers.
five spices. This is a most pleasant, aromatic seasoning containing powdered star anise, fennel, Szechuan pepper, cloves, and cinnamon. Used mostly in fowl and meat dishes. Also known as barbecue powder or heung new fun.
foo gaw. See: melon, bitter.
fun see. See: bean threads.

geem jean. See: lily flowers.
golden needles. See: lily flowers.

hairy melon. See: melon, hairy.
harusame. See: bean threads.
heung new fun. See: five spices.
hoi sien sauce. See: chili bean paste.
hong daw. See: dates, red.

jeung. A sauce.
joke. Congee, a thick soup.

lily flowers. Dried lily flowers used as a flavoring. Known as geem jean or golden needles.
lo buk. See: radish, Chinese.
long rice. See: bean threads.

longans.   The pleasant-tasting pulpy fruit of a tropical tree related to
   the lichii, widely grown in China.
lotus root.   This oddly-shaped, smooth-skinned root, russet-brown in
   color, is segmented every six to twelve inches or so. Inside are sym-
   metrically-arranged holes running the lengh of each segment that
   present a very pleasant design when the root is sliced crosswise. Can
   be simmered, pickled, or stuffed. It has a pleasant always-crisp
   texture and a nice bland flavor.

mee jean.   See: monosodium glutamate.
mei boi.   See: monosodium glutamate.
mei jing.   See: monosodium glutamate.
melon, bitter.   This is very popular during the summer months because
   its slightly bitter taste imparts a cooling effect. It is used in soups,
   steamed, or fried. To prepare, scrape off the skin and remove the
   pulp and seeds. Known as foo gaw.
melon, hairy.   Has a somewhat fuzzy skin which should be scraped off
   like that of a carrot. Used mainly in soups. Known as mow gaw.
melon, winter.   A rather large melon about the size of a pumpkin
   when fully grown. Usually used in soups or steamed. Has a "cold
   air" effect if simmered for several hours. Prepare for use by removing the seeds and the pulp surrounding them. Known as dong gaw.
monosodium glutamate.   A crystalline, water-soluble powder consisting essentially of sodium salt of glutamic acid extracted from the
   protein portion of vegetable sources. It is very effective when used in
   moderation to bring out the flavor of meats, stews, and vegetables,
   but is of no use with baked products, eggs, or sweets. Also known as
   mee jean, mei boi, mei jing, and vetsin.
mow gaw.   See: melon, hairy.

noodles, cellophane.   See: bean threads.
nuts.   Lotus and white nuts are used to impart their distinctive flavors
   to soups.

oriental vermicelli.   See: bean threads.

plum sauce.   A greenish fruit sauce used with poultry dishes.

radish, Chinese.   A winter radish served as a vegetable and often
   used in soups. Known as lo buk.
red bean sauce.   Used as a flavoring. Known as saang see jeung.
red dates.   See: dates, red.

saang see jeung.   See: red bean sauce.
salted fish.   See: fish, salted.

"satin" chicken.   This simply refers to the satin-like texture of this dish.

sauces.   See: plum sauce, red bean sauce, and universal sauce.

sausage, Chinese.   A flavorful mixture of chopped pork seasoned with sugar and soy sauce and then "dried" slightly. It is used as a meat dish or for flavoring other dishes.

shrimp paste.   Ground shrimp stabilized with salt and used to flavor meat dishes.

star anise.   A spice having a star-shaped seed pod. One of the ingredients in five spices.

taro.   A very starchy tuberous root used widely throughout the orient instead of potatoes.

translucent noodles.   See: bean threads.

turnips, preserved.   Usually salted and used for flavoring soups, meat, and vegetable dishes. Known as chung choy.

universal sauce.   A condiment widely used for sea foods, consisting of 1 part fermented black beans (dow see), 1 part fresh ginger root, 1 part fresh garlic, and 2 parts of soy sauce.

vermicelli, oriental.   See: bean threads.

vetsin.   See: monosodium glutamate.

vinegar, Chinese.   Prepared from fermented rice.

water chestnuts.   A pleasant, mildly-flavored, crunchy, bulbous vegetable that can be eaten raw. Retains its crunchiness when cooked.

winter melon.   See: melon, winter.

wun zee.   See: cloud ears.

Index

Abalone—Cantonese 32
Abalone—Oyster Sauce 31
Bean Curd—Fresh with Oyster Sauce, Food value and Protein content 25
Bean Curd—Stuffed with Meat 44
Bean Sprouts—How to sprout 79
Bean Sprouts—with Cod Fish 24
Beef—Ginger 34
Beef—Oyster Sauce 35
Beef—Steamed with Sweet Cucumber 50
Bitter Melon—Stuffed, Vegetable Spaghetti 43
Buns—Steamed, Stuffed, Chinese with Salted Egg Yolks, Barbecued Pork and Sweet Bean Paste 47
Cat's Paws (Har Gow)—A Chop Suey Filling in Rice Dough . 51
Chicken—Almond 59
Chicken—Cantonese 57
Chicken—Curried 26
Chicken—Diced Almond 23
Chicken—Deep Fried Liver and Gizzards 59
Chicken—Golden Needles and Red Dates, Steamed . . . 42
Chicken—Golden Needles and Red Dates, Braised 29
Chicken—Mushroom Velvet 28
Chicken—Peas-in-the-Pod Fillet 26
Chicken—Roast Satin 65
Chicken—Satin Spice 65
Chicken—Steamed Mushroom, Universal Sauce, Etc. . . . 42
Chicken Balls—Mushrooms, Tomato 38
Chicken Balls—Pineapple, Lichee Nuts, Dragon's Eyes . . . 38
Chop Suey—Aristocratic 20
Chop Suey—Beef, Chicken, Pork, Shrimp 19
Cod Fish—Shrimp Sauce 45
Cod Fish—with Bean Sprouts 24
Congee—Beef, Fillet of Cod 71
Congee—Ducks Wing, White Nuts and Tripe 71
Custard—Chinese Sausage, Duck, Salted Eggs 48
Duck—Barbecued 54
Duck—Country Style 62
Eggs—Chicken Foo Yong, Shrimp, Pork, Lobster, Mushroom, Crab Meat 39

Eggs—Fried with Peas 28
Eggs—Hundred Year Old 78
Eggs—Rolls, Egg Roll Batter 58
Eggs—Salted, Steamed with Pork 49
Fish—Fresh Bean Curd 35
Fish—Deep Fried with Tomato Sauce 57
Fish—Stuffed 36
Fish—Sweet and Sour 37
Fish—Satin 64
Fish Cake—Almond 36
Gluten—Beef 34
Gluten—Deep Fried with Tomato Sauce 61
Golden Coin—Chicken and Pork 54
Lobster—Cantonese 30
Lobster—Oyster Sauce 31
Meat Cakes or Balls—Steamed 49
Mushrooms—Steamed, Stuffed 48
Mushrooms—Amino Acid Content 7
Noodles—Chinese Soup 74
Noodles—Cantonese Chow Mein 75
Pork—Barbecued 53
Prawns—Deep Fried 56
Pudding—Almond, Sesame Seed 78
Radish—Chinese with Shrimp 23
Rice—Beef Curried White 74
Rice—Fried with Beef, Sweet and Sour, Tomato, Mushrooms . 73
Rice—Chicken Fried, Pork, Vegetable 73
Rice—Steamed White, How to Cook 72
Sausage—Steamed Chinese, Preserved Pork or Duck,
    Salted Fish 43
Sauces—Served on the Table with Any Meal 17
Sea Cucumber—Steamed, Stuffed 46
Shrimp (Prawns) Balls—Mushrooms 40
Shrimp (Prawns) Balls—Tomato 32
Shrimp—Black Beans (Dow See) 44
Shrimp (Prawns)—Chilied Turnip 46
Shrimp (Prawns)—Deep Fried 56
Shrimp (Prawns)—in Lobster Sauce 40
Shrimp (Prawns)—with Chilied Bean Paste (Hoi Sien Jeung) . 33
Shrimp (Prawns)—with Chinese Radish 23
Soup—Abalone 66
Soup—Bean Curd, Dried Mushroom 70
Soup—Bean Curd, Fresh 69
Soup—Bird's Nest, Shark's Fins 70
Soup—Cantonese Egg Swirl 63
Soup—Chicken Giblet 67
Soup—Eel Maw 69
Soup—Egg Flower Swirl 63
Soup—Fresh Lotus 67

Soup—Lettuce and Fish 66
Soup—Mustard Greens 64
Soup—Sea Cucumber 68
Soup—Subgum 66
Soup—Winter Melon, Bitter Melon, Hairy Melon 68
Spareribs—Barbecued 53
Spareribs—Dried 56
Spareribs—Garlic 29
Spareribs—Red Bean Paste (Saang See Jeung) 30
Spareribs—Steamed Garlic 50
Spareribs—Sweet and Sour 27
Squid—How to Prepare, In Aristocratic Chop Suey 20
Sweet and Sour—Spareribs, Chicken, Chicken Liver 27
Taro—with Black Beans and Preserved Pork 24
Tea—Common Chinese 76
Tomato—with Beef, Sauce 21
Translucent Noodles (Cellophane)—or Fun See 22
Universal Sauce—made from Ginger, Soy Sauce, Dow See
    and Garlic 24
Vegetables—Plain, Fried Cabbage, Hop Choy 22
Winter Melon—Chinese Greens, Mustard Greens 50
Won Ton—Deep Fried, Soup 60
Won Ton Soup 61